Mark
The Gospel of Jesus

Other books by this author:
The Essential Jesus (Editor)
The Fragmenting of Adventism (Pacific Press)
Glimpses of Grace

To order, **call 1-800-765-6955.**
Visit us at **www.reviewandherald.com** for information on other
Review and Herald® products.

William G. **JOHNSSON**

Mark
The Gospel of Jesus

REVIEW AND HERALD® PUBLISHING ASSOCIATION
HAGERSTOWN, MD 21740

Unless otherwise noted, all Scripture passages are from the *Holy Bible, New
International Version.* Copyright © 1973, 1978, 1984, International Bible Society. Used by
permission of Zondervan Bible Publishers.

Texts credited to NEB are from *The New English Bible.* © The Delegates of the
Oxford University Press and the Syndics of the Cambridge University Press 1961, 1970.
Reprinted by permission.
Texts credited to NKJV are from the New King James Version. Copyright © 1979,
1980, 1982 by Thomas Nelson, Inc. Used by permission. All rights reserved.
Bible texts credited to Phillips are from J. B. Phillips: *The New Testament in Modern
English,* Revised Edition. © 1958, 1960, 1972. Used by permission of Macmillan
Publishing Co., Inc.
Bible texts credited to RSV are from the Revised Standard Version of the Bible,
copyright © 1946, 1952, 1971, by the Division of Christian Education of the National
Council of the Churches of Christ in the U.S.A. Used by permission.

This book was
Edited by Gerald Wheeler
Copyedited by Delma Miller and James Cavil
Cover design by Ron J. Pride/square1studio
Cover art by Lars Justinen, GoodSalt.com
Interior design by Candy Harvey
Typeset: 11/13 Bembo

PRINTED IN U.S.A.

08 07 06 05   5 4 3 2 1

R&H Cataloging Service
Johnsson, William George, 1934-
    Mark: the gospel of Jesus.

1. Bible. N.T. Mark—Commentaries. I. Title.
                226.3

ISBN 0-8280-1872-3

Dedication

For everyone
who seeks from the heart
to know the truth about
Jesus of Nazareth

Contents

Introduction

Some time ago the Washington *Post* ran a remarkable article that stretched across three full pages. It wasn't the length of the piece that made it surprising—the *Post* has a reputation for extended coverage—but the tone. Unlike the usual approach of the *Post,* which generated investigative reporting in its exposure of the Watergate scandal, this article had not a trace of cynicism or skepticism. Instead, it carried a sustained air of admiration, almost of adoration.

Titled "The Doctor's Saving Grace," the article was about famous Seventh-day Adventist pediatric neurosurgeon Dr. Ben Carson. Carson, who performs more than 400 operations a year, saving children's lives and bringing hope and relief to so many, had himself been diagnosed with an aggressive form of prostate cancer. The surgery was scheduled that day at Johns Hopkins, where Carson is director of pediatric neurosurgery as well as professor of neurological surgery, oncology, plastic surgery, and pediatrics in the medical school.

The article reported how calls, letters, and e-mails from thousands of former patients and admirers around the world had flooded Carson's home and office. "He can't die," said Shirley Howard, president of the Children's Cancer Foundation. "We need him here on this earth to cure our children with brain tumors."

Dan Angel, a Hollywood producer who with Whoopi Goldberg is planning a film on Carson's life, said that "he performs miracles, and now he needs one."

Faced with the possibility of death, Carson nevertheless continued to operate on others. "What is striking about him—almost overwhelming—is the sense of warmth and calm that seems to radiate from his core. You immediately feel at ease, that he is completely present in the moment, that he cares deeply. At the same time, there's a lightness to him, a quiet good humor, a ready smile," noted the *Post* reporter.

The early diagnosis looked grim: an MRI seemed to indicate that the cancer had metastasized to the spine. Next morning Carson was up very early and walking the dog, reflecting on his life and saying to himself, "You know, I've lived 50 years, twice as long as I ever thought I was going to live when I was growing up. It's been a good life, and if it's time for me to go, OK."

But a spine surgeon, an expert at reading MRI screens, saw Carson's results and told Ben that the pattern came from congenital causes, not metastasized disease. So Carson scheduled surgery to have the tumor in the prostate removed.

The next day's *Post* carried a follow-up story. The surgery had gone well, and the cancer had not spread beyond the prostate. Ben Carson in all likelihood would be able to carry on with his ministry of healing and motivational writing and speaking.

At the close of the long *Post* article, the reporter detailed Carson's help to 15-year-old Caroline Shear, who suffered increasing headaches. The operation to relieve the pressure on Caroline's brain involved difficult work at the base of the skull, but Carson, facing his own surgery and an uncertain future, undertook the task.

A week later Caroline was up and out, happy to be free of headaches. "He's incredible," she said of Carson. "He's so humble. I don't know what it is about him, but he's just like an everyday person you'd see in the grocery store. You wouldn't think he's this world-famous surgeon.

"He's like the closest thing to God, the way he helps people."

What a tribute! "The closest thing to God." Ben Carson is what he is, and does what he does, because of God. He reflects God manifested in humanity, Jesus Christ. Jesus changed Ben from a hotheaded teenager into the gentle, humble Dr. Carson. Two thousand years ago Jesus went about doing good, spending most of His time healing, bringing hope and a new start to men and women and boys and girls that everyone else had given up on. Today, if you want to understand what makes Ben Carson "tick," it is the power and influence of Jesus Christ.

Carson is a shining example of the transforming influence of Jesus, but he is only one of a host. From the time Jesus walked the trails of Galilee up to today, the noblest and best lives our planet has seen have sprung from Jesus.

The Mother Teresas.

The Albert Schweitzers.

The Florence Nightingales.

Jesus, God's Son, came to this earth, showed us by word and deed what God is like, and changed forever the course of human history. Without question He is the most influential person in the roll call of the ages.

His influence embraces people of all ages, all social standings, and all places. No one is too young or too old, too weak or too strong, too poor or too wealthy, too broken or too successful, not to be turned into a new and better person by Jesus.

And, transformed by Him, they change the world into a better, kinder, nobler place.

In this book we still study the life and teachings of Jesus as portrayed by one from the generation when Jesus actually lived—someone who himself also was altered by Jesus. We will see how John Mark sets forth Jesus.

It is a very early portrait, quite possibly the first. And it is dynamic, thrilling: "Jesus, the Son of God." While He is the man of Galilee, He is much more: He is the God-man, the Son of God.

As we see Jesus, we discern what humanity might be—what our lives could be as, like Ben Carson's, His presence transforms them.

I found the commentary by Larry W. Hurtado, *Mark: A Good News Commentary* (San Francisco: Harper and Row, 1983), helpful in the preparation of this book and have referred to it a number of times.

I am indebted to Chitra Barnabas for keyboarding the manuscript.

1

The Beginning of the Gospel
(Mark 1:1-20)

Several years ago an Australian academic, Barbara Thiering, authored a sensational book about Jesus. *Jesus the Man: A New Interpretation From the Dead Sea Scrolls* argued that Jesus did not die on the cross. Rather, He revived, later married Mary Magdalene, fathered three children, then divorced Mary for another woman, and at last died in old age!

What is most amazing is that this fantastic portrayal, which is more fiction than fact, found a reputable publisher (Doubleday). It is, perhaps, the most extreme example of a current phenomenon—the making of Jesus after human images. Depending on the scholar or writer, Jesus comes out as a religious fanatic, a teller of tall tales, a political revolutionary, a feminist, or whatever the particular author set out to find.

Scholars have been probing the historical Jesus—seeking to find out what He was *really* like—for more than 200 years. For the most part, however, their reconstructions have had limited popular impact, circulating mainly among academics. Now the media explosion of our times has stripped away taboos, and no topic or person is off-limits. Jesus Christ has become fair game for analysis, dissection, and critique like any other celebrity.

In this book we intend to take the words of Mark's Gospel at face value. I believe they give us an accurate account about Jesus, and that by studying them we can arrive at a true picture of the historical Jesus.

That is a position that more and more scholars and an increasing number from the informed public would challenge. It seems necessary, therefore, to give some attention as to why we may trust Mark's Gospel, and, indeed, all four Gospels as reliable sources for our understanding of Jesus. After that we shall take a look at the term *gospel* and see how it evolved under the impact of the life and work of Jesus of Nazareth. Finally, we shall probe what Mark meant when he began his account with the phrase "Jesus Christ, the Son of God."

The Reliability of Mark's Account

I believe that we may study the Gospel of Mark, as well as the other Gospels in the New Testament, confidently as trustworthy sources for the following reasons:

1. *The evidence of eyewitnesses:* Luke wasn't one of Jesus' followers so as to be able to draw on personal recollections of the Master, but he went to those who were eyewitnesses. He tells us: "Many have undertaken to draw up an account of the things that have been fulfilled among us, just as they were handed down to us by those who from the first were eyewitnesses and servants of the word. Therefore, since I myself have carefully investigated everything from the beginning, it seemed good also to me to write an orderly account for you, most excellent Theophilus, so that you may know the certainty of the things you have been taught" (Luke 1:1-4).

Luke's Gospel is the first of a two-part work, and in the second, the book of Acts, he again underscores the role of those who had been with Jesus during His earthly life: "After his suffering, he showed himself to these men and gave many convincing proofs that he was alive. He appeared to them over a period of forty days and spoke about the kingdom of God. . . . Therefore it is necessary to choose one of the men who have been with us the whole time the Lord Jesus went in and out among us, beginning from John's baptism to the time when Jesus was taken up from us. For one of these must become a witness with us of his resurrection" (Acts 1:3-22).

The Gospel of John likewise emphasizes the eyewitness nature of its account: "The man who saw it has given testimony, and his testimony is true. He knows that he tells the truth, and he testifies so that you also may believe" (John 19:35). "This is the disciple who testifies to these things and who wrote them down. We know that his testimony is true" (John 21:24).

Mark's Gospel does not directly mention the eyewitness aspect, but he does write it as someone would as they recall the life and ministry of Jesus. This Gospel gives comparatively little attention to the sayings of Jesus, instead stringing together a series of vivid word pictures of Him in action. As we study this Gospel we find that Mark supplies details omitted by Matthew and Luke in relating the same incident. For instance, only Mark gives the actual words spoken by Jesus when He raised Jairus's daughter to life—*"Talitha koum,"* Aramaic for "Little girl, I say to you, get up!" (Mark 5:41). Again, only Mark tells us that in healing the deaf-mute Jesus said, again in Aramaic, *Ephphatha!* meaning "Be opened!" (Mark 7:34).

Although Mark wasn't one of the original 12 disciples of Jesus, he very likely was present for some of the events he describes in his book. Only in his Gospel do we find this intriguing detail from Jesus' arrest in the Garden of Gethsemane: "A young man, wearing nothing but a linen garment, was following Jesus. When they seized him, he fled naked, leaving his garment behind" (Mark 14:51, 52). Is this a reference to Mark himself? It seems likely. Otherwise it's hard to understand why he would mention the young man, who plays no other part in the story.

The book of Acts and the letters of Paul contain several references to Mark, who was also known as John Mark or Marcus. He was the cousin of Barnabas and son of Mary (Acts 12:12, 25; 13:5, 13; 15:37-39; Col. 4:10; Philemon 24; 2 Tim. 4:11; 1 Peter 5:13).

Tradition has it that Mark went to Egypt and founded the church of Alexandria. He became the presiding elder of the church but died during the persecution unleashed by the Roman emperor Nero.

His Gospel, as do the other three in the New Testament, carries the ring of authenticity, the vividness and attention to detail, that only an eyewitness can supply. It comes from someone who was *there* or at least heard from those who were.

2. *The evidence of history:* Early in the second century Papias, bishop of Hierapolis in Asia Minor, gathered information about the origins of the Gospels. Whenever he met someone who had known one of the apostles, he inquired diligently about what Andrew, Peter, Philip, Thomas, James, John, Matthew, or any other of the Lord's disciples had said and done. Papias wrote a work in five books entitled "An Exposition of the Oracles of the Lord."

His work has now disappeared, but other writers quote fragments from it. Thus the first church historian, Eusebius, in his *Ecclesiastical History,* preserves the following from Papias concerning the Gospel of Mark:

"Mark became Peter's interpreter and wrote accurately all that he remembered, not, indeed, in order, of the things said or done by the Lord. For he had not heard the Lord, nor had he followed him, but later on, as I said, followed Peter, who used to give teaching as necessity demanded but not making, as it were, an arrangement of the Lord's oracles, so that Mark did nothing wrong in thus writing down single points as he remembered them. For to one thing he gave attention, to leave out nothing of what he had heard and to make no false statements to them" (*The Seventh-day Adventist Bible Commentary,* vol. 5, pp. 563, 564).

This very early voice out of Christian history affirms the reliability of Mark's Gospel: "Mark did nothing wrong," that is, he made no mistakes. Papias' reference to Peter's being the source for Mark's account accords with the evidence from the Gospel itself: Where Peter enters Mark's narrative, the account becomes particularly vivid (Mark 1:36, 40; 2:1-4; 3:5; 5:4-6; 6:39, 40; 7:34; 8:33; 10:21; 11:20, etc.). Interestingly, Peter, in his letter, calls Mark his "son" (1 Peter 5:13).

3. *The evidence from dating:* In 1985 a self-appointed group of 74 scholars from different seminaries and universities, mainly in the United States, came together under the name of the "Jesus Seminar" to find the "real" Jesus behind the Gospels. Cofounders Robert Funk and John Crossan set out to liberate the historical Jesus from the "myths" that they believe have surrounded Him since the first century. They discarded from the outset any possibility of miracles: no one can cure sick people, nor do dead people (Jesus included) come back to life.

The Jesus Seminar analyzed each of 1,500 sayings attributed to Jesus and voted with colored beads as to whether Jesus really said it or something like it. A pink bead meant He probably uttered it; a gray bead implied that while He didn't say it, the ideas were similar to His; and a black bead indicated that He didn't say it at all.

Their results? Fully 82 percent of the Gospel sayings didn't originate with Jesus. Most of the remaining 18 percent are doubtful, and we can be confident of only 2 percent as authentic! When the Lord's Prayer emerged from the seminar's scrutiny, the only words left were "Our Father"!

Understandably, the Jesus Seminar has received sharp criticism from many scholars. The media, however, have picked up on their results and given them wide (and unwarranted) publicity. This played into the hands of the seminar, which all along has seemed to aim its work at the general public rather than the academic world.

The effect of the Jesus Seminar has been to massively weaken confidence in the Gospels as reliable sources, and thereby in the Jesus that they portray. But the conclusions of the Jesus Seminar, together with similar ones from other scholars in the past and present, fail before one crucial point: the *time* factor.

Whatever their view of the reliability of the four Gospels, scholars date them all within the first century: Mark the earliest in the 60s, Matthew and

Luke in the 70s or 80s, and John in the 90s. Some scholars place Matthew, Mark, and Luke before 70 on the grounds that we would have expected the fall of Jerusalem (in A.D. 70) to be reflected more clearly if the narratives had emerged later.

For several reasons, many scholars consider Mark to be the first of the four Gospels writers. They point out that Matthew and Mark both contain material found in Mark, sometimes word for word. In fact, only 31 verses in Mark have no parallels either in Matthew or Luke. The arguments pro and con about the "Markan priority" get complicated and need not concern us here. The point is that scholars have regarded Mark as written very early—in the 60s at the latest.

But that puts it within a generation of Jesus' ministry, when plenty of people would be still alive to refute it if it were as wildly inaccurate as the critics allege.

Mark's Gospel contains numerous stories of the mighty acts of Jesus—restoring sight to blind individuals, casting out demons, healing those who were deaf and mute, feeding the multitudes, raising the dead, and at last leaving His own tomb empty. How easy it would be for the doubters and critics to stop the new Jesus movement dead in its tracks with: "No way! We saw Jesus in Nazareth in Galilee. He didn't do miracles or walk on water. And you can find His body in a cave in Jerusalem. All those stories about Him are nonsense."

If Mark had composed his Gospel a century later the critical scholars today would have a more reasonable argument. We would have to take seriously their thesis that His followers embellished the story of Jesus, so that the church, not Jesus Himself, originated the sayings attributed to Him. *If* . . . But it wasn't. Mark's Gospel appears 30 years or less after Jesus died on the cross. That's too close to the events to give credence to the critical thesis.

And there is a final piece of evidence:

4. *The evidence from earliest Christian worship:* In Paul's letter to the Philippians, it's as though he suddenly bursts into singing. Notice how the New International Version in its translation tries to capture the poetic form of Paul's words:

> "Your attitude should be the same as
>   that of Christ Jesus:
>   Who, being in very nature God,
>   did not consider equality with God
>   something to be grasped,
>   but made himself nothing,

> taking the very nature of a servant,
>   being made in human likeness.
> And being found in appearance as a man,
>   he humbled himself
>   and became obedient to death—
>   even death on a cross!
> Therefore God exalted him to the
>   highest place
>   and gave him the name that is
>   above every name,
> that at the name of Jesus every knee
>   should bow,
> in heaven and on earth and under
>   the earth,
> and every tongue confess that Jesus
>   Christ is Lord,
> to the glory of God the Father" (Phil. 2:5-11).

In fact, Paul was singing—or quoting an early Christian hymn. We find him doing a similar thing elsewhere, as in 1 Timothy 3:16.

But look again at Philippians 2:5-11 and notice what this very early hymn teaches:

> a. Jesus was God by nature.
> b. He was equal with God.
> c. He became truly human.
> d. He died on the cross.
> e. God exalted Him to the highest place.
> f. He is Lord.

Paul wrote to the Philippians around A.D. 62, and he quotes a hymn with which his readers must have been familiar. How long would it take for a hymn like this to be composed and spread to the church at Philippi? We have no way of knowing, but it's reasonable to conclude that the hymn originated at least 5 to 10 years earlier, maybe much sooner.

What I mean is this: Very, very early in the life of the Christian church the followers of Jesus who were worshipping Him as truly God believed in the Incarnation, proclaimed His death on the cross, and boldly affirmed that He was the risen Lord. That to me is highly significant.

Here are the alternatives: On one hand, the Jesus Seminar and other critical scholars argue that Jesus was no more than a man, a teacher who did no miracles and who died like any other person. The narrative in Mark's Gospel, they say, reflects myths invented by the church. Very well—now, how much time do they need for all this scenario to develop? Way more than they have available!

The alternative viewpoint is that the resurrection of Jesus confirmed to His followers what His words and His miracles pointed to—that He was truly Deity in the flesh. Within a short time they were worshipping Him as God and composing hymns to Him as Lord of all. And Mark's Gospel, like the other three, wasn't an invention of the new religion, but an accurate account of what actually happened with the Man of Galilee.

I have had some acquaintance with "God men." I lived in India and on two separate occasions encountered supposed incarnations—Mehar Baba of Ahmednagar, and Rajneesh of Poona (later of Antelope, Oregon). Both attracted and were revered by international followings. And both claimed divine powers.

But both died.

And both are no more.

Twenty years later you won't find congregations singing hymns to them. Their movements collapsed with their death.

You can take it to the bank: Mark will give you an accurate steer about Jesus.

The Best News

Mark begins his Gospel with gospel, small g: "The gospel of Jesus Christ . . ." (KJV). The Greek word *euaggelion,* usually translated "good news," in fact indicates the best news. It has a fascinating history.

The term itself goes back a long way. In Homer's *Odyssey* it means "reward for good news," but later took on the sense "of good news," especially with regard to victory in battle.

"*Euaggelion* is a technical term for 'news of victory.' The messenger appears, raises his right hand in greeting and calls out with a loud voice: *chaire . . . nikōmen* [rejoice, we have won]. By his appearance it is known already that he brings good news. His face shines, his spear is decked with laurel, his head is crowned, he swings a branch of palms, joy fills the city, *euaggelia* [sacrifices] are offered, the temples are garlanded, an *agon* [assembly] is held, crowns are put on for the sacrifices and the one to whom the message is owed is honored with a wreath" (*Theological Dictionary of the New Testament,* vol. 2, p. 722).

During the first century A.D. the imperial cult (the worship of the Roman emperor as divine) gradually took root. And this very word, *euaggelion,* became connected with it. The people celebrated the accession of the emperor to the throne as introducing a new era that brought peace to the world and was "gospel" for all people. On his death signs in the heavens declared that he had joined the ranks of the gods.

When Christians used *euaggelion,* however, they did not refer to Caesar. For them it referred to another individual, one of lowly birth, a despised teacher who died on the cross, but who rose again from the dead. "Gospel" meant good news of victory, of ultimate triumph over sin, death, and the grave.

What currents of history swirl around this familiar word! On one level Caesar and Christ have much in common—both were hailed as saviors, both were worshipped as God in the flesh—but they belong to different worlds. If Caesar's birth and accession was "good news," Jesus' life, death, and resurrection was the *best* news!

From the ancient Greeks to Caesar to Jesus *euaggelion* developed still further. Writings about Jesus began to appear, quite possibly Mark's being the first. They weren't biographies in the usual sense, because they omitted details we usually expect to find in a biography. For instance, we get no account of what Jesus looked like, and much of His life gets passed over with scant or no mention. Mark, like John, tells us not a word about His birth or adolescence. Instead, all four Gospel writers focus on the three or so years of His ministry, and all give disproportionate space to the Passion Week. And all are more than mere chronicles or reports: they breathe faith. John stated his purpose clearly:

"Jesus did many other miraculous signs in the presence of his disciples, which are not recorded in this book. But these are written that you may believe that Jesus is the Christ, the Son of God, and that by believing you may have life in his name" (John 20:30, 31).

In a startling way Jesus of Nazareth dominates these writings. They are more than good news *about* Him— He *is* the gospel. And so in the course of time the writings themselves became known as Gospels.

Matthew, Mark, Luke, and John weren't the only attempts at writing a Gospel. Luke tells us, remember, that "many" had attempted such a task before he made the effort (Luke 1:1). We have no knowledge of what those other "Gospels" from the first century were like—they did not survive. The Holy Spirit, who had guided the four writers we know about, also superintended in the process of which ones should survive and be included in the canon of the New Testament.

We do know that fascination with the story of Jesus continued to generate other "Gospels" beyond the first century. Some of those later works have survived. They attempted to gain credibility by attributing the writing to one or another of the apostles—falsely so, because the apostles were all long dead. Such "Gospels" often contain some bizarre material. For example, in one the child Jesus already knows the alphabet before His mother begins to teach Him to read. Making pigeons out of clay, He throws them in the air, and they fly! The Gospel of Thomas (but *not* from Thomas) consists wholly of sayings of Jesus. It closes with Jesus stating that a woman must become a man if she is to enter the kingdom of heaven!

One more word about Gospels: the highest form of praise is imitation. Late in the second century, when the story of Jesus had spread far and wide and Christianity had begun to challenge the old order of the Greek and Roman gods, the pagans came out with a counter "Gospel" based on one Apollonius of Tyana, a supposed miracle worker from the previous century. But, written long after Apollonius' time, it failed to make an impact. How could it? There was—and is—only one Jesus, and only one true gospel.

The Son of God

Throughout Mark's Gospel we find the disciples failing to grasp who Jesus really was. Although they were constantly at His side to observe His mighty acts, they seemed blind to the conclusion to which such deeds pointed.

Sometimes we too can be so close to a loved one or a friend that we cannot see the big picture—cannot see who they really are. Only when that person is no longer with us, separated from us by distance or by death, do we wake up and realize the treasure that lay at our fingertips.

Mark tells us that Jesus made a studied effort to avoid publicity, frequently telling people whom He had healed to keep it to themselves (e.g., Mark 1:43-45; 5:42, 43). Although some commentators have argued that Jesus' approach was really a reverse-psychology strategy—if you tell someone *not* to do something, they are more likely to do it—such an explanation seems forced. I think the truth is rather that Jesus deliberately avoided the popular connotations of the Messiah (one who would deliver the Jews from their Roman overlords) and wanted to hold down the public excitement that He knew His miracles would generate.

So in Mark's Gospel especially, Jesus' Messiahship is a secret one. Perhaps the course He adopted puzzled the disciples, for Mark frequently tells us (the readers) that they didn't understand (e.g., Mark 4:13, 41; 6:51,

52; 8:17-21). They were right alongside Jesus, but didn't see Him. Only after the Resurrection did they get it.

Mark wants us to understand, however. He tells us in his opening words that Jesus is the Son of God. Not about to simply report facts about Jesus of Nazareth, he lets us know right off the bat the significance of those facts. The whole story points to one conclusion: Jesus is the Son of God.

In Mark's Gospel, as in the other three, Jesus' favorite designation for Himself is "Son of man." But others keep driving home the point made by the author at the start of his Gospel.

Twice the Father declares that Jesus is His Son—at Jesus' baptism (Mark 1:11) and on the Mount of Transfiguration (Mark 9:7).

The evils spirits cry out, "You are the Son of God!" (Mark 3:11; see also 5:7). Ironic indeed. Although the people and even the disciples fail to recognize who Jesus is, the demons know it and acknowledge Him.

Once Jesus simply calls Himself the Son, over against the Father (Mark 13:32).

At His trial the high priest asked Him, "Are you the Christ, the Son of the Blessed One?" (Mark 14:61). And Jesus replied: "I am" (verse 62).

Finally, the centurion who stood guard at the cross and saw how Jesus died found himself forced to confess, "Truly this man was the Son of God!" (Mark 15:39, KJV).

But what precisely did Mark mean in his opening words? Is Jesus the Son of God because of the Incarnation, or does the title, which, of course, occurs elsewhere in the New Testament, have still deeper meaning?

We are all children of God, His sons and daughters, because He is the Father of all. But Jesus is "Son" in a much different sense. Mark's uses of "Son of God" for Jesus suggest a closeness to God that none of us can claim. When God speaks audibly from heaven addressing Jesus as "My beloved Son," it signifies a unique relationship.

Elsewhere in the New Testament the term *Son* is a key one. Hebrews 1:1-4, for instance, makes three marvelous affirmations concerning the Son. First, He is the radiance of God's glory. The word translated "radiance," *apaugasma,* suggests a beam of light, a bright ray, a shining forth. Various translations render it as "effulgence" (NEB), "brightness" (KJV), "reflection" (RSV), or "radiance" (Phillips). This description lifts us to the realm of glory, where the Son shines in eternal day. Dwelling in light unapproachable, He *is* the Light of lights.

He is also "the exact representation of [God's] being" (verse 3). Here the metaphor changes to the concept of a seal and its impression on wax.

The word is the same as the one from which we derive the word "character," and tells us that the Son is the very stamp of the divine essence. What God is, the Son also is.

But the affirmation of the Son's glory and deity goes further: The Son *is* the divine radiance and the divine essence. Literally, "being"—not became. Eternally the Son is the Light of light, the image of the divine. He has always been so and eternally will be so.

The terminology of Father and Son may mislead us. Inevitably we associate it with time and origin. Sons derive their being from fathers, and a father is prior in time. But Jesus as eternal Son did not originate through the Father. Rather, the biblical language of Father and Son points to shared being, equality, divine essence. And the Jews so understood this language, for when Jesus called God His own Father, it offended them because they realized He was "making himself equal with God" (John 5:18).

Ellen White's statements about Christ's eternal preexistence and deity run along the same lines. While her "in Christ is life, original, unborrowed, underived" (*The Desire of Ages,* p. 530) has become a classic quote, no less significant is the following:

"The Son is all the fullness of the Godhead manifested. The Word of God declares Him to be the 'express image of His person.' . . .

"Christ is the preexistent, self-existent Son of God. . . . In speaking of His preexistence, Christ carries the mind back through dateless ages. He assures us that there never was a time when He was not in close fellowship with the eternal God. He to whose voice the Jews were then listening had been with God as one brought up with Him. . . . He is the eternal, self-existent Son.

"While God's Word speaks of the humanity of Christ when upon this earth, it also speaks decidedly regarding His preexistence. The Word existed as a divine being, even as the eternal Son of God, in union and oneness with His Father" (*Evangelism,* pp. 614, 615).

While affirming the eternal sonship, Ellen White suggests that the Incarnation made Him Son in a different way: "While the Son of a human being, He became the Son of God in a new sense. Thus He stood in our world—the Son of God, yet allied by birth to the human race" (*Selected Messages,* book 1, p. 227).

This, then, is the beginning of the gospel: Jesus Christ is God's Son. All that God is, He is, was, and ever will be. God has come to earth to dwell among us!

2

The Exorcist

(Mark 1:21-2:17)

*I*n today's world many people—even preachers—are no longer convinced that God exists, and they certainly don't believe in the devil as a personal being. But Mark's account of Jesus' life and work confronts such ideas head-on.

According to Mark, Jesus' first public act involved driving a demon out of a human being. It was a Sabbath, and we find Jesus in Capernaum, by the lake of Galilee, teaching the people who had come to worship. That itself is surprising, for Jesus has no credentials—He has not attended the rabbinical schools to be considered qualified in the exposition of the law. Furthermore, Mark tells us that the people that Sabbath morning were amazed at what they heard. Jesus' teachings came clear, crisp, certain, with no qualification, no "Rabbi Hillel says thus . . ." or "Rabbi Shammai, however, explains the Scripture like this . . ."

Suddenly a man shouted in the synagogue, shattering the Sabbath calm: "What do you want with us, Jesus of Nazareth? Have you come to destroy us? I know who you are—the Holy One of God!" (Mark 1:24). And Jesus, abruptly cutting off His discourse, addressed the demon speaking through the man. "Be quiet!" He ordered. "Come out of him!" (verse 25). The man shuddered violently, then shrieked as the devil left him. And now the Sabbath worshippers were even more astonished. "What is this?" they said to one another. "A new teaching—and with authority! He even gives orders to evil spirits and they obey him" (verse 27).

We could hardly imagine a more dramatic opening to Jesus' ministry.

It is the most gripping beginning of any of the Gospels. And the portrait of Jesus that the reader sees from the outset is that of one who confronts and bests the powers of evil. Jesus is the exorcist par excellence.

Such ideas startle the modern Western mind, accustomed as we are to explanations from psychology and psychiatry. They call every believer who seeks to take the Bible seriously and also to keep in tune with the times to an experience of deep reflection. Indeed, there is much in this passage (Mark 1:21-2:17) that invites careful study and discussion. Because of limitations of space we shall confine ourselves to five aspects: (1) the shaping of the respective Gospel accounts; (2) demons and demon possession; (3) the expression "Son of man" that Jesus often used of Himself; (4) His prayer life; and (5) the "messianic secret."

The Shaping of the Gospel Accounts

As we try to understand Mark's portrayal of Jesus, and in particular his initial singling out of the exorcism in the synagogue at Nazareth, we will find it helpful to compare and contrast Mark as Gospel writer with Matthew, Luke, and John.

For 200 years Bible scholars have tried to figure out how Matthew, Mark, Luke, and John did their work. They have found themselves intrigued by the surprising similarities and dissimilarities of the four accounts, especially within the Synoptic Gospels—Matthew, Mark, and Luke. For some years the view prevailed that the four writers worked largely in "scissors-and-paste" fashion, piecing together sayings of Jesus already circulating among Christians with other material to form their respective Gospels.

That understanding of the formation of the Gospels has long since fallen by the wayside. We now know that each writer, inspired by the Holy Spirit, selected from the data at his disposal—personal recollections in the case of Matthew and John, and other sayings and miracles shared collectively by the first followers—and shaped them into a distinctive, individual portrait.

Thus while the four Gospels cover the same ground, and much of the material overlaps, each is a separate and individual account. No one Gospel is sufficient, nor can we dispense with any one. Only as all four portraits come together do we catch the complexity of Jesus of Nazareth. God was behind the process. The Gospels originated at His intent. We find no parallel to them in human literature or religion.

Here are some ways the earnest seeker can grasp the distinctive portrait of each Gospel writer:

1. Read the Gospel in itself, preferably at one sitting, without mingling ideas from the other Gospels.

2. Observe carefully how the Gospel begins. Study the emphasis given at the commencement of Jesus' public ministry—that is, what act or incident does the Gospel writer play up at the outset?

3. Observe how the Gospel closes.

You will find a correspondence between opening, commencement of public ministry, and close in each account. Out of all the materials at each writer's disposal, each selects elements that fit the distinctive, inspired portrait of Jesus that they will craft.

Here's an outline to check out:

Matthew: opens with Jesus Christ "the son of David, the son of Abraham" (Matt. 1:1). We see immediately that the *Jewishness* of Jesus will be the ruling motif of this Gospel. Matthew primarily has a Jewish audience in view. And he wants them to know that Jesus is the Son of David, Israel's long-awaited Messiah.

The ministry commences, not with a dramatic act, but a sermon (the Sermon on the Mount, Matthew 5-7). Five sermons of Jesus shape the Gospel, echoing the five books of the Pentateuch. Thus Jesus is the second Moses, but also one greater than Moses who is in addition king.

At the close Jesus, now the risen Lord, is still teaching. He commissions His followers to make disciples of all nations by going, baptizing, and instructing them (Matt. 28:18-20).

Luke: opens with the writer's dedication of his Gospel to Theophilus (Luke 1:1-4). This approach, common among Gentile writings of the time, indicates that he, in contrast with Matthew, had non-Jewish readers as his target audience.

Jesus' ministry commences with the sermon at Nazareth (Luke 4:16-30). Unlike the Sermon on the Mount, however, the emphasis falls on the words from Scripture (Isa. 61:1, 2) that Jesus quotes: the promise of good news to the poor, freedom for the prisoners, recovery of sight for the blind, and release for the oppressed. Elaborating on the text, Jesus shows how, even in Old Testament times, Gentiles such as the widow of Zarephath and Naaman the Syrian found God's favor. His words infuriate the synagogue crowd, and, thrusting Him outside, they try to kill Him.

The close: Jesus commands His followers to witness to all nations, beginning at Jerusalem (Luke 24:45-49). But this is not really the end of Luke's account, for he adds a part 2, also dedicated to Theophilus (Acts 1:1), in which he recounts how the followers of Jesus did indeed carry the gospel to the world, starting with the Jews in Jerusalem but eventually going far beyond, right up to Rome, the capital of the empire (Acts 28:16, 30, 31).

John: opens with the most sublime words of all the Gospels. "In the beginning was the Word, and the Word was with God, and the Word was God" (John 1:1). His account, John is telling us, is about God—the eternal Creator-God, who for a little while camped among us, becoming a human being, "full of grace and truth" (verse 14).

Jesus' ministry commences with a series of encounters between Him and the men who become His first disciples (verses 35-51): Andrew, Peter, Philip, Nathanael. He speaks one-on-one with each, revealing insights into their character, showing His interest and plans for them. And this will be the pattern of this glorious Gospel: He who is God in the flesh takes time to talk with "good" people and with "bad," with theologians and with beggars, with His mother and with loose women, and with governors and with nobodies.

The close: Jesus is still talking, once again with Peter and John and the others. Gently rebuking Peter, He reinstates him among the apostles, then gives a hint of what lies ahead. The One full of grace and truth, He continues interested, caring, and compassionate to the end of His earthly sojourn. It is a life so amazing, so wondrous, that John says the very world could not contain all the books that humanity might write about it (John 21:25).

And so back to *Mark.* We already noticed how he opens with his key insight that Jesus is the Son of God (Mark 1:1). His ministry commences with a dramatic encounter with the powers of darkness, which reveals that He is indeed whom Mark has claimed. Before Him the demons tremble and give up their captives with shrieks, acknowledging Jesus publicly. Powerful are the forces of evil, but Jesus, Son of God, is stronger!

The close: As we shall notice in a later chapter, the exact ending of Mark's Gospel lies in dispute. The oldest manuscripts of the Gospel stop at Mark 16:8—"Trembling and bewildered, the women went out and fled from the tomb. They said nothing to anyone, because they were afraid." Many scholars think that Mark could not have intended to shut off his account so abruptly, and possibly they are right.

Or wrong. Mark's opening is just as abrupt: "The beginning of the gospel about Jesus Christ, the Son of God." Further, the reactions of people to Jesus, seen at the outset in His exorcism in the synagogue at Nazareth and subsequently throughout this Gospel—amazement, wonder—are exactly those that we find in Mark 16:8.

Demons and Demon Possession

For many Christians in the West, demons and demon possession no longer make sense or have meaning. They have bought into a naturalistic worldview that denies any invasion of the supernatural, in which one can no longer believe in the devil as a personal being and in which even the concepts of "right" or "wrong" have become relativized.

One of the foremost scholars behind the shift in such conceptions was the twentieth-century German theologian Rudolf Bultmann. In a series of books and articles he argued that modern science and psychology made outmoded the biblical accounts of miracles and exorcisms, so the New Testament had to be "demythologized." And the majority of modern scholars, along with large numbers of members from the mainline churches, have adopted Bultmann's worldview.

Before we join the crowd, however, we need to note several salient points.

First, the Bible clearly teaches the existence of a personal being known as the devil or Satan. It argues, especially in the New Testament, that an unseen world exists alongside the one we see and live in. In this invisible world both good and evil beings exist and affect our lives. The apostle Paul states this worldview succinctly: "For our struggle is not against flesh and blood, but against the rulers, against the authorities, against the powers of this dark world and against the spiritual forces of evil in the heavenly realms" (Eph. 6:12).

To attempt to "demythologize" this worldview—to deny its literal reality and to relegate it to just a spiritualized meaning—dishonors and distorts the text. Nor are we here dealing with an occasional text or passage of Scripture. Rather, we face the understanding and work of our Lord Himself. Throughout the Gospels, especially in Mark, we find Jesus confronting demons, speaking to them, silencing them, and commanding them. Indeed, the New Testament in several places portrays His saving work as *Christus victor*—a triumph over the powers of evil: "And having disarmed the powers and authorities, he made a public spectacle of them, triumphing over them by the cross" (Col. 2:15; see also 1 Peter 3:21, 22).

Further, we have to question whether modern thinking has too quickly discarded the concept of the demonic. The century just past saw evil raised to a level and a scale unprecedented in human history: two great wars and scores of lesser ones; atrocities and unspeakable violence; weapons of mass destruction able to wipe out all life on earth; Hitler, Idi Amin, Pol Pot, and a procession of perpetrators of evil that the world can dub only "monsters." If the devil doesn't exist anymore, someone very much like him has taken his place!

This reluctance to admit the reality of demons is a Western character-istic. Elsewhere people have no problem with the concept. I taught for many years at Spicer College in India, and students in my Life and Teachings of Jesus classes not once raised questions about the actuality of the Gospel accounts of Jesus' confrontation with demons. Rather, they re-galed me with similar stories out of their own experience.

What I discovered in India holds true for Africa, Latin America, and elsewhere in Asia. In a major article, "The Next Christianity" (*Atlantic Monthly,* October 2002), history professor Philip Jenkins analyzed the growing tension between "Northern" Christianity (Europe and North America) and "Southern" Christianity (Africa, Latin America, Asia). He notes: "Of course, American reformers also dream of a restored early church; but whereas Americans imagine a church freed from hierarchy, su-perstition, and dogma, Southerners look back to one filled with spiritual power and able to exorcise the demonic forces that cause sickness and poverty. And yes, 'demonic' is the word. The most successful Southern churches today speak openly of spiritual healing and exorcism" (p. 60).

For Seventh-day Adventists, demons and demon possession do not present a problem. We read the canvas of history in terms of a cosmic war-fare, the great struggle between Christ and Satan. The conflict took on heightened intensity at the first coming of Christ as the forces of evil mar-shaled their strength and cunning in an effort to thwart His mission to bring salvation to the world. That is why we see Jesus so often in direct conflict with demons in Mark's account.

We also believe that at the close of human history—just before Jesus comes again—Satan and his hosts will redouble their efforts to keep cap-tive the world that he claims as his own. Thus even while many people in the West today deny that demons even exist, they are nevertheless caught up in a battle for the mind, for allegiance to either Christ or Satan.

And, as Jesus triumphed over the evil powers at His first coming, so will He emerge victorious in the end-time.

The Son of Man

In Mark 2:10 we encounter for the first time in the Gospel the phrase "Son of Man," when Jesus says to the teachers of the law: "But that you may know that the Son of Man has authority on earth to forgive sins." The expression, which occurs a total of 14 times in Mark, is Jesus' most common designation for Himself throughout the Gospel. Interestingly, nowhere do we find anyone else applying the term to Him.

Jesus' use of "Son of Man" is intriguing. It sounds unusual to us, to say the least. For instance, the president of the United States does not say: "The president has decided that . . ." Obviously Jesus chose the expression with care as He sought to convey to His followers and to the people in general who He was and the nature of His mission.

But what did Jesus mean by "Son of Man"? Biblical scholars have engaged in fierce debate, producing scores of articles and books on the topic, but they have failed to come to any consensus as to its meaning. While a number seek the answer in the nonbiblical writings associated with the period of the New Testament, I think the biblical roots of the expression provide the key.

We find the expressions "a son of man" or "sons of man" often in the Old Testament with the sense of "man," a "mere man," or "human beings" (e.g., Ps. 8:4; 144:3; 145:12). Throughout the book of Ezekiel God addresses the prophet as "son of man" (e.g., 2:1, 3, 6, 8). However, Ezekiel does not use the term of himself. All these Old Testament occurrences of "son of man" clearly underscore the *humanity* of the designee.

In the book of Daniel, however, we find a single usage that appears in a striking context: "In my vision at night I looked, and there before me was one like a son of man [KJV: "the Son of man"], coming with the clouds of heaven. He approached the Ancient of Days and was led into his presence" (Dan. 7:13). Here we observe "son of man" applied to a particular being in heaven who is given authority, glory, and power, and who is universally worshipped (verse 14).

These Old Testament uses of "son of man," it seems to me, provided Jesus with a self-designation that accurately fit His person and mission. Through the Incarnation Jesus truly had become one with us—He was the Son of *man,* bone of our bone, flesh of our flesh. But He was *more than* just a human being. He came from heaven and returned to heaven, in the process winning back the world for God, so that at length at the name of Jesus "every knee should bow, in heaven and on earth and under the earth, and every tongue confess that Jesus Christ is Lord, to the glory of God the Father" (Phil. 2:10, 11).

Jesus was Israel's long-awaited deliverer, the Messiah, and when Peter declared Him to be it, Jesus did not correct him (Matt. 16:16, 17; note that "Christ" is the Greek equivalent of the Hebrew word "Messiah"). But by Jesus' time expectation had become focused on Messiah's role as one of bringing victory over the hated Romans, who occupied the land. However, Jesus steadfastly renounced the political function of His mission, refusing to head up a revolutionary movement that would drive out the invaders by force. That, presumably, is why He avoided use of the loaded term *Messiah* for Himself.

Although Larry Hurtado in his commentary on Mark fails to connect Jesus' use of "Son of Man" with Daniel 7:13, he captures the essence of the term: "This son of man, this human, is in fact not just another human, but exercises divine authority. The usage of the term reflects the whole message of Mark, that the man Jesus is in fact the Son of God (1:1; 15:39). Without attempting to deal here with all the issues concerning the history of the use of the term, we may safely conclude that the term as used in Mark describes Jesus as a human being who is not recognized for who he really is. The term *the Son of Man* is the 'outward' or 'public' title, which expresses no special or obvious dignity in itself. But, because we have been informed already (1:1) what Jesus' real significance is (the Son of God), we see the irony of the title. The title conveys the scandal of Jesus, that this mere man (in the eyes of his uncomprehending contemporaries) should teach and act with such radical and shocking authority" (Larry W. Hurtado, *Mark,* p. 24).

Jesus' Prayer Life

In Mark 1:35 we find a revealing picture of Jesus: "Very early in the morning, while it was still dark, Jesus got up, left the house and went off to a solitary place, where he prayed."

Jesus had had an extremely full day. He had taught in the synagogue, cast out demons, and healed Peter's mother-in-law. After sunset the people crowded around Him—"the whole town," says Mark—with their sick and demon-possessed. And Jesus gave Himself unstintingly to help alleviate the pain and suffering.

We don't know when Jesus got to bed that Saturday night, but it must have been late. Did He, exhausted, drop off to sleep at once? Or did the excitement of the day cling to Him still, His mind reliving episode after episode? Whatever the case, the night was a short one for Him. Maybe a few hours of sleep, perhaps five at most, but well before dawn He was up and out of the house, making His way by the pale light of the stars to a lonely place.

For Jesus, prayer was more important than sleep. In a succinct statement Ellen White captures the role of prayer in His life and ministry: "His humanity made prayer a necessity and a privilege. He found comfort and joy in communion with His Father. And if the Savior of men, the Son of God, felt the need of prayer, how much more should feeble, sinful mortals feel the necessity of fervent, constant prayer" (*Steps to Christ,* p. 94). Privilege we readily grasp, but *necessity?* Only as we catch the force of that element do we realize that Jesus was truly one with us in frailty and weakness, facing the same struggles and tests we face and needing the same divine help that we must have in order to overcome.

Mark mentions Jesus praying at two other times: after feeding the 5,000 (Mark 6:46) and in Gethsemane (Mark 14:32-39). Luke, however, records eight occasions Jesus prayed (Luke 3:21; 5:16; 6:12; 9:18, 28; 11:1; 22:32, 41), noting that on one occasion Jesus spent the entire night in prayer (Luke 6:12).

How negligent are we who profess to follow in Jesus' steps! Foolishly, we think we can live the Christian life and do the Lord's work in our own strength. We have time to eat, drink, and sleep; time to shop and party; time to watch TV and read the newspaper—but we are "too busy" to pray. In truth, we are really too busy *not* to pray. We spend countless hours in committee meetings but spend only moments with the Lord. Although we plan and discuss and make budgets, we do it in our limited strength and out of our imperfect wisdom.

The Lord's way is so simple, but it is the only one that will bring success in our Christian living or ministry. Simple—and yet difficult. Because to truly pray is to confess one's helplessness, to cast oneself on the Lord's strength, to invite and permit Him to take over the heart and the work. And that is hard for our proud selves to let happen.

Notice one more aspect from Mark's account: the need for a quiet time and place. In today's frenetic, crazy world it's become increasingly difficult to find quietness. More and more people, it seems, cannot bear silence—anywhere or anytime. They have to fill every moment and every space with sound—and even louder sound. Why are they afraid of the silence? Could it be that they don't want to give opportunity to the One who says: "Be still, and know that I am God" (Ps. 46:10)?

I believe that times of silence are absolutely necessary for mental and spiritual health. Alone and quiet, we may look deep within ourselves and discover who we are and in the process become comfortable with ourselves. And alone and quiet, God speaks to us the wonder of His love and the mysteries of His purposes for us. All the great men and women of faith have known and followed this regimen of quietness: Enoch who walked with God, Abram communing with God under the starlit skies, Moses in the desert of Midian, David the shepherd boy watching over the family flock, Esther seeking divine guidance and strength prior to appearing before the king on behalf of her people, the young man Isaiah praying in the Temple, the administrator Daniel praying in Babylon, Martin Luther rising in the early hours, Ellen White at her desk long before the dawn, and so on.

And Jesus, rising very early after a short rest, going out to a solitary place and seeking His Father's will.

The Messianic Secret

Three times in Mark 1:21-2:17 the writer tells us that Jesus "amazed" those who saw and heard Him. The worshippers in the synagogues were astounded at His teaching (Mark 1:22) and then amazed at the exorcism (verse 27), while those who witnessed His healing of the paralytic lowered through the roof were also amazed (Mark 2:12).

As we move deeper into Mark's Gospel we will find that His own disciples likewise continually responded in surprise at what Jesus said and did. At times His actions terrified them. Again and again they failed to grasp who He was and what He had come to do. This is true right to the end. Although He tells them that He is going to Jerusalem, where He will be rejected, scorned, beaten, spat upon, and killed, and then rise again, they seem bewildered. They don't get it.

But others do—not human beings, but the demons. In Mark 1:24 the demon cries out through the lips of the man whom it possesses: "I know who you are—the Holy One of God!" We find demons making similar statements frequently in Mark's account.

His Gospel weaves the story of Jesus in a highly dramatic account around the question of who He is. To the crowds He is a man who says and does the incredible, while to His followers He is wonderful but mysterious, not fitting the mold of their preconceived ideas. As the Gospel proceeds, the tension builds, reaching a climax in the rejection and crucifixion in Jerusalem—and then the empty tomb.

To the reader, however, the story of Jesus plays out on a different level. The reader knows from the outset what neither the crowds nor the disciples grasp—that Jesus is "the Son of God," or at least that is what Mark believes and understands to be the key to unlocking the mystery of this enigmatic figure.

The Gospel of Mark, then, is like a detective story. Mysteries, a genre at which British writers seems to excel, typically describe a crime, scatter clues as to "whodunit," and dangle several suspects before the reader. The author leads the reader on a journey of discovery with the detective, who eventually unmasks the murderer. Only at the very end does the reader get it. Occasionally, however, mysteries follow the opposite course: the reader knows the murderer from the outset, and the interest lies in following the detective as he or she methodically uncovers how the crime was committed and at last confronts the murderer. It is the approach followed in the *Columbo* television series (I doubt that it could be made to work in print, however).

In the Gospel of Mark we see both formats operating simultaneously. The Gospel is a mystery, the conundrum of Jesus: "Who is this?" ask the disciples (Mark 4:41), while Jesus Himself asks them: "Who do people say I am?" (Mark 8:27); "Who do you say I am?" (verse 29). For the people and the disciples, the mystery of Jesus gradually discloses itself, although even by the end few actually "get it." The book closes with even His followers amazed, trembling and bewildered, not yet understanding and believing. But for the reader, the mystery is solved from the outset—if he or she chooses to accept Mark's opening words. The Gospel as it proceeds thus unfolds what Jesus as Son of God is like in word and deed, and what His mission to earth involved in purpose and experience.

Jesus is the Messiah, but the secret Messiah, rejecting the acclaim and the expectations popularly associated with the term. To the crowds and—for most of the time—He is an intriguing but puzzling miracle worker who breaks conventions and dies a horrible death. But to the believer, the one who "gets" it, He is Messiah in truth, God's Son come down to work out eternal salvation for the world.

3

Man of Controversy
(Mark 2:23-3:35)

I have a problem with most of the pictures of Jesus we see in print: Jesus looks soft and effeminate. They belong to a tradition that goes back a long way—perhaps to the cloisters in which monks, shut away from the world and engrossed in lives of prayer and contemplation, portrayed Jesus after their own pale-faced likeness.

But the Jesus of the Gospels, and of Mark's Gospel in particular, was anything but a weak character. Tanned by a life spent largely outdoors, with muscles toned from hard physical work, He could easily drive merchants and money changers out of the Temple, overturning their tables as He flailed a rough-made whip. We see Him frequently engaged in argument with the religious leaders over His word and actions. He is a man of controversy.

> "Gentle Jesus, meek and mild,
> Look upon a little child . . ."

It's a lovely prayer, but misleading. Gentle He was indeed—gentle enough to lead His flock like a shepherd and carry the lambs in His arms (Isa. 40:11), and meek, if we realize that "meekness" for Him did not mean becoming a doormat but the emptying of self-will and ambition. But "mild"? No way. A mild Jesus would not have been perceived by the religious and political establishment to be enough of a threat for them to begin, early in His ministry, to plot how they might kill Him, as we find in the passage of this chapter (Mark 3:6). A mild Messiah would not have ended His life executed on Calvary.

Throughout the second and third chapters of Mark the dominant theme is controversy. We have already seen Jesus in conflict with the teachers of the law over His forgiving the sins of the paralytic lowered through the roof (Mark 2:6, 7), His going to the party thrown by Levi-Matthew (verse 16), and His failure to encourage His followers to fast (verse 18). Now we will study four more incidents that place Jesus at the center of conflict: the disciples' plucking and eating grain on the Sabbath (verses 23-28), Jesus' healing a man with a withered hand on the Sabbath (Mark 3:1-6), the accusation that He was in league with the devil (verses 22-30), and the tensions within His own family circle (verses 20, 21, 31-35).

Controversy Over the Sabbath

The Gospels record seven Sabbath miracles of Jesus (John 5:1-15; Mark 1:21-28; Mark 1:29-31; Mark 3:1-6; John 9:1-41; Luke 13:10-17; Luke 14:1-4). In each case He healed someone, and in each case the person was not in an emergency situation or condition.

Further, His Sabbath healings all took place publicly, sometimes with the teachers of the law present to witness them. Understandably, what they regarded to be flagrant Sabbathbreaking incensed the teachers, and sharp disputes often resulted from the miracles.

The fact that Jesus could have avoided much controversy if He had chosen a different track is undeniable. He could have waited until after sundown or taken the sick aside and healed them privately. Obviously He chose to make the Sabbath and His relationship to it a defining feature of His mission.

We need to look carefully at Jesus' actions and words in relation to the Sabbath, seeking to figure out why He took the course He did in fulfilling His mission. And we must also stand back and view His actions and words in light of the entire witness of Scripture—not in a defensive manner, but keeping in mind that *"all* Scripture is given by inspiration of God" (2 Tim. 3:16, KJV) and that each part sheds light on the others.

Many Christians, without very much study of the Bible or the history of the early church, think that Jesus abolished the Sabbath. But the big picture shows just the opposite. He Himself said: "Do not think that I have come to abolish the Law or the Prophets; I have not come to abolish them but to fulfill them. I tell you the truth, until heaven and earth disappear, not the smallest letter, not the least stroke of a pen, will by any means disappear from the Law until everything is accomplished" (Matt. 5:17, 18). The Sabbath, after all, predates the Fall of humanity. It has its roots in Creation, not salvation. Because Jesus is our Savior, the Sabbath means *more* to us than it does to the Jews—never any less.

In Jesus' conflict with the religious teachers over the Sabbath, whether it should be kept or which was the day of rest was never an issue. What was at stake was *how* people should observe the Sabbath. Jesus, by word and deed, broke with the longstanding traditions surrounding the Sabbath, setting it in a new and—to the scribes—uncomfortable framework. And that in turn turned the spotlight on Jesus' authority. Who He was and what right He had to set aside the rabbinical regulations was the real issue behind the Sabbath controversies.

For the Jews the Sabbath was perhaps the supreme demonstration of loyalty to God. Some later rabbis held that if all Israel would but keep the Sabbath twice, Messiah would come. So the Pharisees, who were sticklers for law, understandably found themselves upset by the conduct of Jesus and His disciples. The religious leaders had elaborated the Sabbath commandment of Exodus 20:8-11 into a complex set of religious customs. These "hedges" around the commandment existed only in oral form in Jesus' day, but later the rabbis codified them into 39 types of activity (in the tractate "Sabbath" in the Talmud) covering regular work, travel, and preparing and eating food.

The Pharisees viewed Jesus and the disciples' going through the grainfield (Mark 2:23, 24) as not merely out for a stroll but as breaking the regulation against traveling on the Sabbath. Further, by picking heads of ripe grain, rubbing off the chaff, and eating the kernels, the disciples also broke the law by gathering and preparing food.

Jesus gives an enlightening response to the critics. At first sight He seems to justify one "sin" by another one: He cites the example of David and his men, who ate the consecrated bread that only the priests were supposed to consume. And He adds: "The Sabbath was made for man, not man for the Sabbath" (verse 27).

By His words Jesus radically reorients the purpose of the Sabbath. The teachers of the law had encumbered the Sabbath command with a host of minutiae that made it into a burden instead of a delight. Jesus came to liberate men and women from physical, mental, and spiritual bonds. Inevitably, in the process He challenged the shackles of tradition associated with the Sabbath.

The words are so simple that we easily fail to grasp the radical shift they bring. The Old Testament calls the Sabbath "My [God's] holy day" (Isa. 58:13). Now Jesus is making it humanity's day. It is still God's day, God's holy day, but it is *ours,* also: a day of rejoicing, a day of freedom, a day of praise, a day of blessing.

But there is more. Jesus' reference to David and his men goes far beyond a rather lame excuse by citing someone else who violated a rule. The point of the Davidic citation is that the king, a fugitive from the wrath of Saul although the anointed future ruler, and his men were on a mission (see 1 Sam. 21:1-6). Hungry and hurried, they came to the tabernacle at Nob and asked for food. The priest had nothing to give them except the consecrated bread that had just been replaced with fresh-baked bread. Although normally only the priests ate the leftover bread, the desperate need of David and his men overrode the rule.

And Jesus is on a mission with His disciples. They travel on the Sabbath as He carries out that mission. It overrides the barriers to Sabbath travel specified by the religious teachers. Likewise with the foraging for grain: the disciples are hungry, and the needs of the disciples as they join with Jesus in mission negate the rabbinical rule.

But the real issue is Jesus, not the Sabbath. The Sabbath is merely the point of contention that brings the true concern into sharp focus. What about this Jesus? Does He have authority to reorient understanding of the Sabbath? Does He have a mission that justifies setting aside the traditional rules regarding Sabbath observance?

The passage that follows immediately (Mark 3:1-6) brings the decision about Jesus to razor sharpness. It is set in the synagogue, the most common religious institution of Judaism in Jesus' time or ours. He addresses the religion of the day, confronting it with His claims and His message. The question is not whether the sick should receive help on the Sabbath—not one of giving humanitarian aid or not—but the actions of Jesus. Are they good or bad? And is His message with its implicit claim for who He is a valid one?

"The urgent ministry and message of Jesus about the approaching Kingdom of God is the immediate context of this story. Mark 3:1-2 suggests that his critics already suspected what he would do, and the Gospels contain other accounts of Sabbath healing by Jesus (Luke 14:1-6; 13:10-17; John 5:2-18; 7:22-24; 9:1-17), leading us to suspect that Jesus may have deliberately healed on the Sabbath as a sign of the significance of his works. That is, his healing on the Sabbath linked his miracles with a day that symbolized for ancient Jews the future Kingdom of God, when bondage would cease and the time of joy and messianic celebration would begin. His Sabbath healings then were to be seen as foretastes and signs of the Kingdom he confidently announced. Further, of course, by healing on the Sabbath Jesus forced people to make a decision about his works and message; for if he had not been called by God to herald the coming Kingdom, if he was not what his Sabbath healings claimed him to be, then he was a Sabbath-breaker. In any case, he could not be written down as simply another harmless religious healer. He prevented that by the way he conducted his healings, making them an issue" (Hurtado, p. 36).

Controversy Over Jesus' Power

Mark 3:20-35 contains a story within a story. It begins and ends with an account of the attitude of Jesus' family to Him (verses 20, 21, 31-35), with the criticism by the teachers of the law over the source of Jesus' power coming in between. We find a similar narrative technique elsewhere in Mark's Gospel (Mark 5:21-42; 6:7-32; 11:12-25).

The scribes who had come down to Galilee from Jerusalem, presumably to spy on Jesus, raised a vicious accusation against Him. "He is possessed by Beelzebub!" they charged. "By the prince of demons he is driving out demons" (Mark 3:22). Beelzebub (or Beelzebul, as some manuscripts read) probably arose from the ancient name of a Canaanite god, Baalzebul, which meant "lord of the high place." We find mention of the god in 2 Kings 1:2-6, 16. Here the term is Baalzebub, "lord of the flies"—perhaps a deliberate Jewish corruption to cast scorn on the rival deity to Yahweh.

That the teachers of the law resorted to such an accusation shows the impact of Jesus' miracles. His exorcisms were so many and of such a dramatic nature that His critics could not deny them. They could respond only that He was in league with the devil.

The other Gospels make clear that the religious leaders frequently brought the same charge against Him (Matt. 12:24; Luke 11:15; Matt. 9:34; John 7:20; 8:48, 52; 10:20). Indeed, the view of Jesus as a sorcerer had a long history in Judaism in the *Toledoth Jesu*. (In modern times, however, many Jewish scholars present a more favorable interpretation.)

Jesus' reply to the accusation exposes its illogic. He gives two short illustrations—a house divided and a kingdom divided—to argue that if Satan is using Him to cast out devils, he is working against himself and will come to an end. No, Jesus' exorcisms cannot result from the devil's power. Rather, they indicate that one stronger than Satan is setting his captives free.

In concluding His defense, Jesus makes a statement that has troubled many Christians: "I tell you the truth, all the sins and blasphemies of men will be forgiven them. But whoever blasphemes against the Holy Spirit will never be forgiven; he is guilty of an eternal sin" (Mark 3:28, 29).

In my first work as a church employee I served for several years as a dean of boys and Bible teacher at a boarding school high in the mountains of India. Most of the students were sons of missionaries, and one day one of them came to see me, deeply troubled. "Sir," he said, "I think I have committed the unpardonable sin. God no longer hears me when I pray. I try to talk to Him, but at the end I don't feel any different."

"Jack [not his real name]," I replied, "you haven't committed the unpardonable sin. The fact that you feel troubled that you might have done so is itself evidence that you have not. A person who commits that sin no longer feels a desire for God or is concerned about their relationship with Him.

"And as for God not seeming to hear your prayers, you are relying on your feelings. Feelings let us down—we can't depend on them. But faith is greater than our feelings. When we pray in the name of Jesus, believing, God *does* hear and answer, regardless of whether we feel different or not. Sometimes feelings accompany God's answer to our prayers, but often we are not aware of any change. That really doesn't matter, because God always keeps His promise to us."

Larry Hurtado captures Jesus' meaning: "The saying in 3:28-29 distinguishes between saying evil things against the Holy Spirit and all other sins, in that there is no forgiveness for the former. The idea of an unforgivable sin has haunted the minds of sensitive people in all Christian centuries, but all such anxiety is misdirected. As the context makes plain, Jesus' warning is against disregarding his message by calling it Satanic (see esp. 3:30), a quite specific deed. A person doing such a thing would have no concern about Christ's forgiveness for it. So, the very anxiety lest one may have done something that cuts one off from Christ's forgiveness is, ironically, evidence that one believes Christ to be sent from God, and thus proof that one cannot have committed the sin warned against here" (p. 51).

In Ellen White's classic on the life of Christ, *The Desire of Ages,* she includes an additional insight about the motives of Jesus' critics:

"The Pharisees to whom Jesus spoke this warning did not themselves believe the charge they brought against Him. There was not one of those dignitaries but had felt drawn toward the Savior. They had heard the Spirit's voice in their own hearts declaring Him to be the Anointed of Israel, and urging them to confess themselves His disciples. In the light of

His presence they had realized their unholiness, and had longed for a righteousness which they could not create. But after their rejection of Him it would be too humiliating to receive Him as the Messiah. Having set their feet in the path of unbelief, they were too proud to confess their error. And in order to avoid acknowledging the truth, they tried with desperate violence to dispute the Savior's teaching. The evidence of His power and mercy exasperated them. They could not prevent the Savior from working miracles, they could not silence His teaching; but they did everything in their power to misrepresent Him and to falsify His words. Still the convicting Spirit of God followed them, and they had to build up many barriers in order to withstand its power. The mightiest agency that can be brought to bear upon the human heart was striving with them, but they would not yield" (p. 322).

Her words give me pause. The Bible warns us that in the last days demonic forces will be at work, with signs and miracles that would, if possible, deceive God's people. Jesus tells us to be on our guard lest we be swept up in the display of counterfeit power (Mark 13:22, 23). His counsels in Mark 3:28, 29, however, provide an important counterweight. It seems to me that, while staying alert, we should be slow to assign anyone who performs miracles or exorcisms to being in league with the devil. They may be, but they also may not. Satan is the accuser. Let's leave the work of accusations to him, while we do the work God has appointed to us—proclaiming the good news.

Controversy in the Family

Although the evaluation of Jesus' ministry by His own family members was not as vicious as that of the teachers of the law, it was nonetheless harsh. "He is out of his mind," they said, and they decided to take action. They would remove Him from the crowds pressing around Him and take control of His life (verses 20, 21).

The incident reveals a high degree of tension in the family. It exposes how different Jesus was from His brothers and sisters and how far apart was their concept of God's will for His mission from His. To we who believe, who have accepted that Jesus was the Son of God and our Lord and Savior, the family's viewpoint seems startling and almost incomprehensible. At the same time, however, it reinforces our sense that Mark is telling us the truth as he shares information that we do not expect.

Did Jesus' mother agree with the family sentiment that He was out of His mind? We cannot tell. Verse 21 simply assigns it to "his family." But

Mary did go along with Jesus' brothers when they went to take Him home and take charge of His life (verse 31). Perhaps Mary, bewildered and unsure of what should be done, simply went along with the plan. Elsewhere Scripture portrays her as pondering the meaning and mission of her remarkable child Jesus (Luke 2:19, 51), so the decision to change Jesus probably originated with the brothers rather than with her.

Elsewhere Mark tells us that Jesus had four brothers: James, Joseph, Judas, and Simon. He also informs us that there were sisters, but does not name them (Mark 6:1-3). Counting Jesus, the family had at least seven children, and this fact has given rise to considerable speculation. It especially puzzles those who follow Roman Catholic dogma and Eastern Orthodox tradition that holds that Mary not only was a virgin at Jesus' conception (as Protestants believe) but remained forever a virgin, never having sexual relations with her husband and therefore never bearing any children after Jesus. This tradition arose early in Christianity under the influence of ideas of celibacy, poverty, and other forms of self-denial that had gained a following among believers. Centuries later the perpetual virginity of Mary became official teaching of the Roman and Eastern branches of the church.

Those who hold to the "perpetual virginity" dogma have to explain Mark's information about Jesus' brothers and sisters. They argue that they were either children of Joseph, Jesus' father, from a previous marriage or cousins of Jesus. The latter view seems rather weak.

The first view has merit (without ascribing to the perpetual virginity of Mary). In the family council of Mark 3:21 we find no mention of Jesus' father. He surely would have taken the lead in reaching a decision and in the attempt to wrest Jesus away from the crowds if he were still alive. Mark's silence concerning Joseph speaks volumes. I believe that we can rightly assume that he was dead by then. Further, the manner in which the brothers of Jesus relate to Him suggests strongly that they were older than He (not only here but in John 7:3-5).

Putting together the information and hints from Scripture, we gather a fairly clear picture of Jesus' family. Joseph, Jesus' legal but not biological father, was an older man at the time of His birth. A widower, he already had several children from his first marriage. Mary was much younger than he, possibly only 16 or 18 or even younger at the time of their marriage. She may have given birth to other children with Joseph as their father. Certainly she did not forever remain a virgin.

Every family has its own dynamics, with affections, hurts, and resentments. Each child forms their own perspective while growing up in the family, often storing up memories of pain and perceived slights or injustices that other members never noticed or long since have forgotten. The family is the crucible of personality, shaping us for good and for ill.

We know enough to conclude that Jesus didn't have a childhood free of pain or an adult family relationship exempt from tension. In *The Desire of Ages* we find this insight:

"Being older than Jesus, they [His brothers] felt that He should be under their dictation. They charged Him with thinking Himself superior to them, and reproved Him for setting Himself above their teachers and the priests and rulers of the people. Often they threatened and tried to intimidate Him; but He passed on, making the Scriptures His guide. . . . Jesus was misunderstood by His brothers because He was not like them. His standard was not their standard" (pp. 87, 88).

The actions of Jesus' brothers as recorded in Mark 3, then, simply continued a pattern established long before. It was time to take this younger brother, who all along had been so difficult to understand, in hand.

But Jesus didn't budge. When told that His mother and brothers were summoning Him, He let them stand outside and went right on doing what He was doing. He loved the members of His family, but He loved God more—and those who opened themselves to God's will. Looking around on those seated in the circle, He said: "Here are my mother and my brothers! Whoever does God's will is my brother and sister and mother" (Mark 3:34, 35).

Now we better understand Jesus' call to discipleship. When He said, "Anyone who loves his father or mother more than me is not worthy of me; anyone who loves his son or daughter more than me is not worthy of me" (Matt. 10:37), He spoke from personal experience. He who had to face the hostility of the religious leaders of His day endured an even sharper pain—rejection by His own family members.

4

The Galilean

(Mark 4:1-5:43)

S everal years ago the Israeli tourism agency in New York contacted my office. In fact, they kept calling, but I was always unavailable. Nor was I in a hurry to get back to them when my assistant Chitra Barnabas told me they were offering a free trip to Israel. I have learned that "free" offers invariably have strings attached, and I did not intend to get caught up in any situation that might compromise my work.

One day, however, Edna Rosenblum, the head of the agency, got through to me. She was putting together a group of Christian editors and writers for a tour of the Holy Land, she said, and she would very much like me to be part of it. The Israeli government would be responsible for all expenses, including airfare.

There had to be a catch. But although I probed deeper and deeper, I couldn't find it.

"Will you expect me to write an article or articles for my publication?" I asked.

"No. Naturally we hope you'll write about Israel, but that will be up to you."

"Will you want to see anything I might write before it goes into print?"

"No. We'd appreciate a copy of what you publish, but that's up to you."

As we talked and talked, I softened. I even asked about food plans, and she replied, "Vegetarian is no problem. I am a vegetarian myself."

So I went to Israel, flying on a packed jumbo jet out of John F. Kennedy International Airport direct to Tel Aviv. There the group assembled. It was a diverse, interesting bunch: two editors of Roman Catholic papers, the editor of the Orthodox paper for North and South America, the managing editor of the *Christian Science Monitor,* a fundamentalist preacher from the South, and a Seventh-day Adventist.

For eight days we traveled around Israel in a white minivan—the six guests with host Edna Rosenblum, who came on the flight from New York, plus a driver cum guide. It was an unforgettable, enthralling experience—a highlight of my life.

I had never visited the Holy Land. Although I had taught college Bible classes for 12 years, with the Life and Teachings of Jesus my most popular course (I wrote the workbook for it at Spicer College), and although as professor of New Testament at the seminary at Andrews University I had led ministerial students in the study of the Gospels, I had not seen Israel. I required students to draw maps that traced the ministry of Jesus, but all I knew about the land where He walked came from books. How I wished I might actually go there and see and feel *His* country!

In God's goodwill it happened, and it didn't cost me a cent. I have been back and would return at the drop of a hat, unstable as the area has become. Without hesitation I say: If you get the chance to go to the Holy Land, take it!

My first impression of Israel was how small a country it is. You travel from Tel Aviv on the Mediterranean to Jerusalem in only an hour or so. Continue east, and you go over to Jericho and the Dead Sea in even less time. And in the process you have crossed the Holy Land from west to east. Going north to south it's longer, but not greatly so. This country, the scene of so many battles and so much bloodshed; sacred to Jews, Christians, and Muslims; the cockpit of the Middle East—it is tiny.

But it seems infinitely varied. The landscape changed continually: hills, valleys, fertile plains, rocky slopes, and desert. But the pearl—the crème de la crème—is the area around and west of the great lake of the Jordan, the Galilee. We spent most of our time there, and after it the Via Dolorosa and the Church of the Holy Sepulchre in Jerusalem were a big letdown.

Jesus was a Galilean. Although born in Bethlehem, just outside Jerusalem, He grew up in Nazareth in the north. By the norms of the Jerusalem establishment He was a provincial, a rustic. "This is Jesus, the prophet from Nazareth in Galilee" (Matt. 21:11), shouted the crowds as He rode a donkey into Jerusalem on His last visit to Judea. But for the religious hierarchy His Galilean origins imposed a significant barrier. "How can the Christ come from Galilee?" they asked (John 7:41).

Today Galilee is a land of beauty and charm where the ancient abuts the modern, where shepherds still watch their flocks by night, but also where you see miles of mangoes and avocados, date palms and bananas—and ostrich farms!

Galilee—it was *His* land. The prophet Isaiah had cried: "Land of Zebulun and land of Naphtali, the way to the sea, along the Jordan, Galilee of the Gentiles—the people living in darkness have seen a great light; on those living in the land of the shadow of death a light has dawned" (Matt. 4:15, 16).

In Mark 4 and 5 we see Jesus in His home country, bringing light in the darkness, rolling back the night. Every one of the incidents in these chapters happens with the lake as a point of reference: He teaches *by* the lake; He calms a storm *on* the lake; He *crosses* the lake to set free just one demon-possessed man; and He *sails back* and restores a suffering woman and a dead girl.

Teaching by the Lake

In Mark 4:1-34 the biblical author for the first time gives us some specifics of Jesus' teaching. Through most of his Gospel he tells of Jesus' miracles and exorcisms, usually in detail, and simply mentions that Jesus preached and taught.

Mark emphasizes that Jesus instructed the people through parables. "He did not say anything to them without using a parable" (verse 34). Why Jesus used the parable format and His goal in doing so are matters that invite our careful consideration.

First, we should notice that the parables of Jesus have a distinctive character. Both before and after Jesus' time sages and writers have looked to the lessons taught by nature, or they have taken incidents from daily life to illustrate moral or religious truth.

But Jesus' parables are different. They aren't teaching aids any more than they are quaint tales with a moral. If we compare them with Aesop's fables or wise sayings such as we find in the book of Proverbs, the contrast hits home. In fact, nothing quite like them appears in Jewish writings or elsewhere. Although couched in simple language and easy to grasp on the surface, they have an existential quality, an immediacy that still strikes home to us today.

Not surprisingly, biblical scholars have invested a great deal of effort in trying to account for Jesus' parables. While they have gleaned some help-ful insights, they have devoted much of their attention to speculations about what He actually said. Holding, as most of them do, that many of the words attributed to Jesus in the Gospels originated not with Him but later in the early church, they try to reconstruct the earliest form of the parables. For reasons that I will not elaborate here, I do not accept this skeptical view of the Gospels. As a result I shall focus on what the Gospels themselves—and in particular Mark's Gospel—reveal about Jesus' parables.

One of their features is the element of surprise: at first glance the story seems simple and straightforward, but it ends with a twist, like an O. Henry tale. Thus in the parable of the workers in the vineyard (Matt. 20:1-16) those who labor for only one hour receive the same wages as those who put in a full day of work. Again, in Jesus' famous parable of the prodigal son (Luke 15:11-32) the story ends with a party—but with the older, "good" boy standing outside in a pout while his ne'er-do-well of a brother is inside having an enjoyable time.

That's one of the reasons for the timeless appeal of His parables. They don't conclude as we might expect. Instead, they end with a "catch" that not only delights but causes us to think.

The surprise ending in the stories often involves a reversal of fortunes or status, as in the parable of the rich man and Lazarus (Luke 16:19-31). Here, the beggar goes to Abraham's bosom, while the rich man winds up in Hades. Several times Jesus has made the parable's point that He summarizes elsewhere: "But many who are first will be last, and many who are last will be first" (Matt. 19:30).

We shall notice below the element of surprise in the parables of Mark 4. It is a feature frequently overlooked in studies of them. First, however, we should observe the role of the disciples in these teachings. Although Matthew and Luke record much of the teaching we find in Mark 4, it is Mark who emphasizes the *secret* nature of the truth revealed by the parables.

When the twelve ask Jesus the meaning of the parables, He replies, "The secret of the kingdom of God has been given to you. But to those on the outside everything is said in parables" (verse 11). Then Jesus quotes Isaiah 6:9, 10, which describes people who see but never get it, who hear but don't understand (verse 12). That is, the disciples are the "insiders" who are supposed to "get it"—the meaning of the parables—while the majority of the people on the "outside" hear Jesus' words as merely interesting tales but little more.

What is the mysterious quality of the parables, the "secret" to which Jesus referred? We find the answer from Jesus Himself: "The secret *of the kingdom of God* has been given to you" (verse 11). So this is what the parables are really about: the kingdom of God—not moral teachings or lessons from nature, but God's activity breaking into human existence in the person and work of His beloved Son. In two parables in this chapter Jesus makes the link explicit: "This is what the kingdom of God is like . . ." (verse 26); "What shall we say the kingdom of God is like . . .?" (verse 30).

Now we begin to understand what the parables meant to the twelve (Jesus' inner circle) and why they still speak so powerfully to humanity—to us!—today. For the twelve, who above all people had the privilege to see the manifestation of divine love and power in their Master, the parables expressed the nature of Jesus' mission. He had come to set up a kingdom (He was indeed Israel's long-awaited Messiah), but that kingdom was poles apart from the sort the crowds wanted and were expecting. It was as far removed as armies, swords, and killing are distant from seed sown in the ground or a sheep lost on the mountains.

Unfortunately most of Jesus' hearers didn't "get it." Even the twelve had to ask Him to explain. Nor do most people today, after so long a time and so many sermons, books, and videos, understand them. For only she who has eyes to see gets it, only he who has ears to hear knows who Jesus of Nazareth is and why He came to earth.

But Jesus called out then and calls out still: "He who has ears to hear, let him hear" (Mark 4:9). Thus the parables, disarmingly simple in vocabulary and plot, pierce home with existential thrust. Do *I* have ears to hear? Do *I* get it? These are the questions about ourselves that the parables force us to face.

Although nearly 2,000 years have passed since Jesus told His parables by the Lake of Galilee, they still ring with excitement and urgency. God is doing something new: the kingdom is breaking in, because Jesus, Son of God, has come to earth! The kingdom seems lowly and insignificant, but it will grow and spread with irresistible power.

It was true then, and is still true. The good news about Jesus is the most powerful force in the world.

Now for a closer look at the well-known parable of the sower and its element of surprise. I have long regarded it as teaching the various types of hearers of the gospel, shown by the different types of soil into which the seed fell. Thus understood, the thrust of the parable falls on failure rather than success. Only after we read of the three places where the seed did not produce a crop do we learn of the soil where it took root and flourished.

A knowledge of ancient methods of agriculture helps us understand the parable and opens up insights. Unlike modern methods in which the farmer first plows the soil and then plants the seed in furrows, the old way was to scatter the seed on unplowed ground and then dig it in. That is why the seed in the parable seems to go everywhere.

The seed that landed on the path, on rocky ground, or in the thorn-bushes came there by accident, not deliberate placement. Most of the seed, however, fell where the farmer intended—on good ground. By concentrating on the three unproductive soils, we imply that the sower's work was largely wasted, but it was not.

And further (here is the surprise), not only did most of the seed yield a crop, but the harvest was wonderfully abundant. The average yield from the ancient agricultural method in Palestine was seven and a half times, with a tenfold harvest considered good (Hurtado, p. 58). But the seed in Jesus' parable resulted in 30-, 60-, and even 100-fold increases, numbers that the farmers who heard the parable could have thought of as only miraculous.

What good news for every gospel worker, then and now! Too often we focus on difficulties and small results, but God concentrates on grace and abundance. No wonder the twelve had a difficult time understanding the parable. So do we. Our faith is too small, our goals too limited. The kingdom of God—irresistible, unstoppable—bursts the bounds of human expectations. So weak and insignificant it seems to be, but like the mustard seed, it grows into a large plant.

Miracles by the Lake

After telling us about Jesus' teaching by Galilee, Mark relates four powerful miracles that run from Mark 4:35 to Mark 5:43. He gives each in detail. Each grips the reader, and the cumulative effect leaves the reader voicing the disciples' question, "Who is this?" (Mark 4:41).

The first miracle in the series, the calming of the storm, shows Jesus' power over nature. The Lake of Galilee is not a large body of water, but it was and still is dangerous. Ringed by high mountains (except where the Jordan enters and leaves), the lake lies 700 feet below sea level. Strong winds come up suddenly and sweep across its surface as heavy masses of air slide down the slopes around it, transforming the body of water quickly from an idyllic calm to a foaming cauldron.

As Mark paints the scene, the contrast between Jesus and everyone and everything around Him could hardly be greater. Caught in howling winds and angry waves, the little boat struggles to stay afloat. Each new wave that crashes over it threatens to send it to the bottom. For the disciples it's their worst nightmare. Some of them sail and work the lake as fishermen, and they know that others of their trade died on a night like this. Those who follow a different profession have heard the stories of men who drowned in these waters, and they too are terrified. We're going down! Down in the darkness, down in the water, down to our death.

And in all this terror, where is Jesus? He lies asleep on a cushion! Exhausted after a day of heavy ministry, the Savior rests. The winds shriek and the waves crash and the disciples cry out in fear, but He reposes in the calm of His Father's love.

The disciples can't comprehend that He can be asleep, can't believe that He is doing nothing as they are about to sink. They wake Him up and in a tone of rebuke demand, "Teacher, don't you care if we drown?" (verse 38).

Are we any better than they? When the storms of life crash around us, we accuse God of doing nothing, of being asleep at His post. "Why don't You *do* something, Lord?" we exclaim. "Don't You care?"

But He does care. And He never fails us. "He will not let your foot slip—he who watches over you will not slumber; indeed, he who watches over Israel will neither slumber nor sleep" (Ps. 121:3, 4). He calls us to trust Him, to wait on Him, to let Him be Lord of our fears.

Then Jesus got up, rebuked the wind, and commanded the waves, "Quiet! Be still!" (Mark 4:39). And the wind died down. Suddenly the sea became calm. The nightmare was over.

"Who is this? Even the wind and the waves obey him!" asked the disciples of one another (verse 41). Perhaps they remembered that in the Old Testament only the Lord Himself ever rebuked the sea. Jesus had just assumed the prerogatives of the God of Israel Himself.

Who is Jesus? He is the Lord of heaven and earth, the Lord of nature—the Son of God.

So they crossed the lake, arriving on the eastern shore in the region of the Gerasenes—today known as the strategic Golan Heights in modern Israel's wars. Jesus and the disciples weren't there long. Although they get out of the boat (Mark 5:2), within an hour or two they climb back in and head across the lake again (verse 18). The reason? The people asked Jesus to leave. In fact, they pleaded with Him to go away (verse 17).

Jesus had performed a wonderful miracle, restoring a wild and crazy man to sanity, but the Gerasenes weren't impressed. In the course of His encounter with the demon-possessed man He gave the devils permission to enter a herd of swine. The herd took off at full speed, plunged over the cliff, and drowned in the lake.

The Gerasenes could not see past the loss of their pigs. Forget that this Man had given a demon-possessed individual his life again—He had destroyed the swine, and they didn't want Him around. "Clearly, in view of the wonderful deliverance of the man, the destruction of the pigs is intended by Mark as insignificant except as an indication of the destructive power overcome by Jesus. But (and here Mark's penchant for irony emerges again) the people seem to be more bothered by the loss of the pigs than happy over the reclaiming of the man, and they ask Jesus to go (5:17). So, the crowd, which went out to see what had happened, saw only the loss of some property—only dead pigs, not the living miracle before them—and not the significance of Jesus shown in the miracle. This lack of perception on the part of the crowd is reflected also in the way Mark describes the response of the people to the former demoniac's proclamation of Jesus' deed (5:20). As noted already . . . , Mark characteristically describes the response of people to Jesus' ministry as amazement. But, though this term connotes the powerful impression made by Jesus' ministry, it is Mark's way of describing a response that is considerably short of genuine faith and insight into Jesus' person" (Hurtado, pp. 69, 70).

As incredible as the Gerasenes' value system strikes us today, it still exists. When the chips are down, most people choose pigs over people. Again and again the weakest among us—the poor, children, the unborn, the sick, the elderly—get thrust aside or sacrificed on the altar of human greed and selfishness.

The Gerasenes begged Jesus to leave, and He did. He never stays where He isn't welcomed, then or now.

Before the disciples weighed anchor, however, He gave instructions totally out of keeping with His ministry up to then. "Go home to your family and tell them how much the Lord has done for you, and how he has had mercy on you," He told the healed man (verse 19). Previously He had always commanded—sometimes sternly—those whom He had restored to keep the miracle quiet. But that was in Galilee, where the people were hoping for the Messiah to appear. The Gerasenes, however, were Gentiles (hence the pig raising, something Jews did not do), and knew very little about Jesus or Messiah. Jesus wanted them also to hear the good news, so if they were scared of Him, He would use the former demoniac as His instrument to reach them.

It worked. When Jesus returned to the area some time later, the people flocked to Him (Matt. 15:29, 30).

Jesus' stilling of the storm on the lake showed His power over nature, while the encounter among the Gerasenes demonstrated His dominion over demons.

The latter incident was every bit as terrifying as the former. This wild, unkempt fellow roamed the mountainside with tattered clothes and broken chains on his hands and feet. The demons who controlled him had full sway. At times he'd grab stones and smash them against his body.

No wonder people feared to pass that way. I'd be scared also. But not Jesus. He who commanded the wind and the waves "Quiet! Be still!" spoke again. The demons fled, and the raging ceased. (Again, the disciples might have remembered that the Old Testament portrayed the Lord as the only one with power over Satan and the forces of evil.) When the local people cautiously came to check out the swineherds' tale, they found the wild man of the mountains sitting quietly, dressed, and rational (Mark 5:15).

So far as we know, Jesus' trip to the Gerasene country was all for the sake of this one person. He healed no one else, presented no teachings—simply restored one sad lost soul to wholeness. What a Savior!

Who is this who commands the demons and they flee? Who is this who travels across the water to a people who reject Him in order to rescue one individual?

Who is He? He is the one who spoke and the world was created, who brought order out of chaos. He is Jesus, the Son of God.

Mark continues his account of Jesus' miracles by the Lake of Galilee, and our wonder increases. With each incident the stakes grow bigger, the tension higher. In Mark 5:21-43 we find another story within a story. A synagogue ruler, Jairus, approaches Jesus, falls at His feet, and begs Him to come to his home to save his daughter, who is close to death. Jesus starts out with Jairus but on the way gets delayed by a woman who has had a bleeding problem for 12 years. She makes her way through the crowd and touches His cloak. Immediately her bleeding stops. As she seeks to slip away unnoticed in the crowd, Jesus calls her back. He wants her and the crowd to know that she hasn't been healed by magic. "Daughter, your faith has healed you," He says. "Go in peace and be freed from your suffering" (verse 34).

We can imagine Jairus' distress as the minutes tick by. He thinks only of his daughter at the point of death, and every moment that passes adds to his fears. Then the worst happens: he gets the dread word that it's too late—she is dead. But Jesus overhears the conversation and comforts the grief-stricken father: "Don't be afraid; just believe" (verse 36). They continue on their way to Jairus' home, where Jesus thrusts aside the wailing mourners. Taking Peter, James, and John, and the girl's parents with Him, He enters the dead girl's room, takes her hand, and says, "Little girl, I say to you, get up!" (verse 41). And she stands up and starts to walk around.

With the woman who had the bleeding problem, Jesus showed His *power over sickness*. Now He demonstrates His *power over death*.

Jesus must have performed many more miracles than Mark recorded, so with profit we may try to figure out why the Holy Spirit prompted him to select the ones he did. What did Mark see in this story within a story with its double miracle? Some connections jump out: both miracles involve women and the number 12, the woman suffering for 12 years, Jairus' daughter being 12 years old.

But there is more: both involve ritual impurity. Because of her bleeding the woman was unclean, defiling anyone or anything she touched: "When a woman has a discharge of blood for many days at a time other than her monthly period, or has a discharge that continues beyond her period she will be unclean as long as she has the discharge, just as in the days of her period" (Lev. 15:25). Likewise the dead girl: "Whoever touches the dead body of anyone will be unclean for seven days" (Num. 19:11).

Thus we can consider the two people Jesus helped in Mark as the lowest of the low. Both were females, regarded by that society as inferior to men. A synagogue prayer from the first century has the worshipper thanking God that he was not born as a dog, a Gentile, or a woman. And these two people weren't only women—they were ceremonially unclean, defiling anyone who touched them.

But Jesus permitted the woman with the bleeding to touch Him. We hear no rebuke, no suggestion of "Keep away from Me!" or "Don't you know you're unclean?" And in the case of the young girl, Jesus reached out and took the dead hand in His.

The regulations of the clean and the unclean had a place in God's purpose for Israel. He intended that thereby His people would learn the difference between the sacred and the profane, that they would discern His holiness. "Be holy, because I am holy" is the constant refrain of Leviticus (Lev. 11:44, 45; 19:2; 20:7). Such ceremonial laws seem to have particularly centered upon the tabernacle and its rituals. They acted as hedges to safeguard the holy.

But such regulations, along with the ceremonial system they served, could have no lasting value. They were shadows, types, parables, all pointing to the One who would come, pitching His tabernacle among us and at length dying on the cross as God's perfect sacrifice for our sins.

Thus the touch of a bleeding woman did not—could not—defile Jesus, any more than His hand on the corpse of a 12-year-old girl.

Who is this, before whom the sickness of the years flees away? Who is this who raises a young girl from the dead? And who is this who cannot be defiled by contact with the unclean?

It is Jesus, the giver of life. Jesus, who rules over both dead and living. And it is Jesus, the one altogether pure and holy.

5

Flash Point

(Mark 6:1-7:23)

*E*ver find yourself in a situation in which anything you say will make you look stupid? A man I know who was invited to be the honored guest at a reunion encountered this thrust from the master of ceremonies: "At what point in your life did you realize you were a genius?"

What can you say to a jab like that? The questioner designed it for laughs—and succeeded. But it also had a sharp edge, a reminder to the guest that he wasn't really better than those in the audience who knew all about him.

Familiarity breeds contempt. Jesus, whom the crowds in Galilee flocked to see, hear, and touch, got a cold reception in His own home-town. "All right, genius, put on a show for us. Do some of the tricks that they say you do elsewhere. You may be able to fool other people, but you can't fool us. We know all about you, so don't try to pull the wool over our eyes."

As with us, Jesus must have craved acceptance by those who knew Him best—or who thought they knew Him best. Their rejection stung. But He didn't argue with them, didn't try to impress. He simply went else-where, leaving the little people of Nazareth to their own little world and little minds.

And elsewhere the Galileans mobbed Him. This portion of Mark, which begins with the Nazareth disappointment, brings Jesus to the height of His popularity, with the crowds convinced that He is the long-looked-for deliverer and ready to declare Him their king. For weeks and months the expectation and enthusiasm have built. What an emotional roller-coaster ride for Jesus! But into this packed, fascinating account Mark inserts a flashback to the death of John the Baptist. His description, longer and more detailed than in any other Gospel, tells us almost more than we want to know. It depicts the decadent feast at which John loses his life. The chef's pièce de résistance is the head not of a boar but of a human, still dripping blood!

We might work through the several incidents one by one in Mark 6:1–7:23 and find much of interest and value. Instead, we shall focus on some of the characters portrayed in the passage. We encounter Jesus' brothers, James, Joseph, Judas, and Simon; Herod Antipas; Herodias, Herod's scheming second wife; Salome, Herod's stepdaughter; the Pharisees and scribes who argue with Jesus over ceremonial cleanness; and so on. But we shall concentrate on the leading players—John the Baptist, the disciples, and He who dominates throughout Mark's Gospel, Jesus of Nazareth, the Son of God.

John the Baptist

Recounting lust, intrigue, violence, and grisly humor, the story of John the Baptist's death provides the stuff of soap operas. But Mark didn't pen it to pass on a juicy tale to his readers. Rather, he had a particular purpose related to his ongoing portrayal of the life and ministry of Jesus.

In the main the Gospel accounts stand on their own, with only occasional echoes from the historians of the time. Here, however, in the story of John's death we find corroborating details in the writings of Josephus, the first-century Jewish historian. Josephus tells us of the Baptist's arrest and attributes it to Herod's fear of a revolt incited by John. He mentions the outrage caused by Herod's marriage to Herodias, because Jewish law expressly forbade a man to marry his brother's wife while the brother was still alive (Lev. 18:16; 20:21). The Baptist's public denunciation of the marriage would have brought more than annoyance to Herod Antipas and his new wife. It would have further stirred up the anger of the people against their ruler.

Herod Antipas was one of the sons of Herod the Great, who tried to catch and kill the infant Jesus. Named tetrarch of Galilee by the Romans in 4 B.C., Antipas ruled until A.D. 39, when he was banished by the emperor Caligula. Herodias, daughter of Aristobulus, was Antipas' niece and about 40 when Antipas took her from his brother Philip and made her his wife. Mark does not mention the name of the girl whose sensuous dance aroused the king's passion, but from Josephus we learn that she was Salome, the daughter of Herodias from her first marriage. The tradition of Salome's dance involving seven veils, however, has no basis in fact.

From one standpoint, Mark's story in chapter 6 describes a scene of ancient Near Eastern decadence. Herod's stepdaughter—probably in her early teens—dances before a banquet of drunken men. The girl knows the sort of performance the king and his cronies will respond to, and gives them a suggestive, sensual display. In his drunken stupor he offers her anything she asks for, up to half the kingdom. Only a fool speaks like this. And he is a fool: mother and daughter have cynically conspired to exploit his moral weakness. The story is one more chapter out of the Herodian sagas, which overflow with immorality, intrigue, and bloodshed.

From the standpoint of John the Baptist, however, the account throbs with tragedy. John, by Jesus' own word, was one of the noblest persons ever to walk the planet (Luke 7:28). Even Herod recognized him to be "a righteous and holy man" (Mark 6:20). God raised up the Baptist to be the Messiah's forerunner, pointing the people beyond himself to One greater who would soon appear. John's preaching—fearless, direct, uncompromising—aroused great interest, so much so that some of his hearers wondered aloud if he were himself the Messiah. But John squashed all such talk. When Jesus commenced His ministry, John saw the crowds thin out and go over to Jesus. The Baptist's disciples complained about the shift, but not John. This humble servant said only: "He must become greater; I must become less" (John 3:30).

Whether preaching to soldiers or tax collectors or standing before Herod, John spoke without fear or favor. If he had followed political expediency, he need never have come to such a tragic end. But then he would have failed the Lord as His appointed messenger.

Mark records that some people were claiming that Jesus was Elijah (Mark 6:15). The final words of the Old Testament predicted that Elijah would return at the end of time: "See, I will send you the prophet Elijah before that great and dreadful day of the Lord comes. He will turn the hearts of the fathers to their children, and the hearts of the children to their fathers; or else I will come and strike the land with a curse" (Mal. 4:5, 6). Through the years Jewish expectation had transformed the prophecy into an anticipation of a great final prophet—either Elijah himself or someone like him—who would prepare Israel for Messiah's kingdom of righteousness.

But Jesus wasn't the Elijah of prophecy. Later Mark records Jesus' experience on the Mount of Transfiguration, when Elijah and Moses met with Him. As they were descending the mountain, Peter, James, and John asked Jesus about the belief current at the time. Apparently they wanted to know if Elijah, whom they had just seen on the mountaintop, would come back to live and work among the Jews. Jesus, however, set them straight: "To be sure, Elijah does come first, and restores all things. . . . But I tell you, Elijah has come, and they have done to him everything they wished, just as it is written about him" (Mark 9:12, 13; see verses 2-11).

John the Baptist, not Jesus, fulfilled the Elijah prophecy. He was no Elijah redivivus but a person whose message, courage, and life bore striking resemblances to the towering figure of the Old Testament. It seems that Mark, especially in chapter 6, underscores the parallels between the two figures.

Both opposed an evil ruler—Ahab on the one hand, notorious for leading Israel down the wrong path, and the decadent Herod Antipas on the other. Each spoke out boldly and publicly in condemning the monarch's evil practices. Toward both the ruler in question had an ambivalent relationship, angry at being exposed but aware that the prophet spoke from God. Both Elijah and John had to deal with a wicked queen who plotted to have them eliminated—Jezebel in Elijah's case, Herodias in John's. And both were men of the wilderness, living much of the time away from society and suddenly appearing to give a message of impending judgment.

Mark's purpose goes even further, however. Surely it is significant that he devotes more space to John the Baptist's death than to his life! At the opening of his Gospel he describes John's message and work in a brief paragraph (Mark 1:2-8). But in chapter 6 his account of the Baptist's death is three times longer. Why? Because Mark ultimately is interested in Jesus, not John, and the death of John points to what lies ahead for Jesus. A shadow falls over His ministry in Galilee, popular though it be—the shadow of a cross.

Jesus knew what lay ahead. The shameful end suffered by John pointed inexorably to the fate awaiting Him. On the descent from the glorious mount He made the connection specific. Explaining that John the Baptist fulfilled the Malachi prophecy and that "they have done to him everything they wished" (Mark 9:12), He inserted a prediction of His own end: "Why then is it written that the Son of Man must suffer much and be rejected?" (verse 12).

The Disciples

Throughout the various incidents that Mark records in Mark 6:1-7:23

we find the disciples at Jesus' side. In some cases they do not enter into the story—they are simply there, spectators, as, for example, when Jesus returns to Nazareth and His own people give Him the cold shoulder.

Elsewhere, however, the disciples play a major role, and they emerge in both positive and negative light. In Mark 6:7-13 we discern a significant extension of the Master's ministry and the disciples' part in it as Jesus sends them out two by two. For months they have been with Him and observed His manner of working. Now the time has come for them to try their own hand.

His instructions make clear that the disciples were to do just what He would do if He were with them. He gives them authority over evil spirits, and they find they are able to drive out "many demons" (verse 13). Like Jesus, they preach that people should repent. And like Him, they heal many sick people.

Jesus sent them out dependent on others for their lodging and daily bread. He told them to take nothing for their journey—not even a sandwich or a snack, no money, no extra clothing. They would find someone to welcome them in each village, someone to care for their needs.

I expect that this part of Jesus' instruction was the hardest for the disciples to obey. They were a group of strong individuals, used to caring for themselves and, at least in the case of Peter, to telling others what to do (he owned several boats and hired workers; see Luke 5:6, 7). Now to set out without any provisions or money, any arrangements for lodging—they must have found that hard.

Everyone who would do God's work, whether as a church employee or not, must still learn the hard lesson of letting go and depending on God. The lesson cuts across all that we have grown accustomed to think and do as we make our way through life. It's the very opposite of how we *want* to operate. But go to the heart of Christian service in any age, and you find this principle: "Apart from me [Jesus] you can do nothing" (John 15:5). " 'Not by might nor by power, but by my Spirit,' says the Lord Almighty" (Zech. 4:6).

And the disciples obeyed. Self-sufficient Peter; shrewd, calculating Matthew; Thomas the skeptic—all went out, preaching, driving out demons, and healing the sick. And the Lord provided as He had promised.

Mark's account of this experience puts the disciples in a wholly positive light. We hear not a word of doubt about the plan or of boasting after the demons yield to them.

But after they return to Jesus the picture changes abruptly. Jesus takes them away in a boat to a quiet place so they can rest and reflect on their first experience in ministry. However, the retreat spot begins to fill with people who have gotten wind of Jesus' destination and run on ahead to it. And so Jesus, instead of enjoying a much-needed break, once again begins to teach the crowd.

It's getting late, and the disciples come to Him with a word of advice. He hasn't realized that the day is nearly gone—the people ought to leave right away and buy something to eat.

But He answers: "You give them something to eat."

What! That would take eight months of a laborer's wages! And where would they find enough food—even if they had enough money?

Despite their experience of only days before when they went out depending on God to provide, the disciples now could reason only according to the old familiar pattern—human solutions. They failed to grasp that One greater than a mere human had the answer at His fingertips before they even became aware of the problem.

Everybody received a hearty meal. In fact, the place overflowed with food, so much so that the disciples gathered up 12 baskets of broken pieces of bread and fish. In the hands of the Son of God a lad's lunch grew and multiplied and fed a multitude.

All four Gospel writers record this miracle—it is the only one that they all mention. Not only was it a dramatic, spectacular event; it marked a turning point in Jesus' ministry. John shares this additional insight: "After the people saw the miraculous sign that Jesus did, they began to say, 'Surely this is the Prophet who is to come into the world.' Jesus, knowing that they intended to come and make him king by force, withdrew again to a mountain by himself" (John 6:14, 15).

We can imagine the elation of the disciples. At last the Master, whom they loved and followed, would receive the acclaim He deserved. It seemed the greatest day of their lives.

But now their emotions suffer a rude jolt. Refusing to accept what the crowd wants, Jesus abruptly sends them home and orders His disciples to get into the boat and leave.

What is it with Jesus? they wonder. *Who is He really, after all? Where is He taking us?*

Keenly disappointed, disillusioned, angry, and frustrated, they set sail. But before long their grumbling ceased as they battled for their lives against a strong headwind. The dead of night, the hours just before the dawn, found them stuck in the middle of the lake. Then they saw a light, a form, moving across the face of the lake, drawing close to them. It was Jesus walking on the water! Thinking it was a ghost, they cried out in terror, but He spoke peace to their hearts: "Take courage! It is I. Don't be afraid" (Mark 6:50).

As Jesus climbed into the boat with them, the wind died down. As Mark notes: "They were completely amazed, for they had not understood about the loaves; their hearts were hardened" (verses 51, 52).

Now we see the real meaning of the miracle of feeding the 5,000. Spectacular it was and extraordinary—but far more. The miracle revealed the secret of Jesus' person. He was more than a miracle worker, more than a healer, more than an exorcist, more than the Messiah of popular longing: He was the Son of God.

And the disciples, for all their time with Him and despite having gone out and preached and healed in His name, still didn't get it.

Jesus

We turn now to consider the events of Mark 6:1-7:23 from Jesus' perspective.

In dealing with the incident at Nazareth, Mark frames his account with the word "amazed." Jesus comes to Nazareth and begins to teach in the synagogue on the Sabbath, and many are amazed (Mark 6:1, 2). But at the close of the story Jesus is Himself amazed because of the stubbornness of heart and lack of faith of the town's inhabitants (verse 6).

Throughout Mark's Gospel we have found that Jesus' mighty works astound people. To be amazed at Jesus, however, falls far short of having faith in Him. To this day many find Jesus interesting, His teachings exemplary, His life noble and uplifting—but they don't believe in Him as Savior. They will readily call Him a good man or wise or even the best that ever lived—but they turn from confessing Him to be God's Son.

And Jesus was amazed at the people of His own hometown. They saw Him grow up among them, knew the purity of His life. All of them had heard the gracious words that fell from His lips and had received reports from near and far how He restored sight to those who were blind, gave hearing to those who were deaf and speech to those who were mute, and restored maimed and broken bodies. But they could think of Jesus only as one of them, no better and no more special.

Even the members of His own family shared the skepticism, as Jesus' words make clear: "Only in his hometown, among his relatives and in his own house is a prophet without honor" (verse 4). Rejection by His loved ones must have especially pained the Savior.

In the negative response of the people of Nazareth we notice an expression without parallel in Jewish writings. They call Jesus "Mary's son" (verse 3) instead of the customary link to His father. The term casts a slur on the circumstances of His birth. In effect, it says, We know he was Mary's son, but who his father was, nobody knows. Later Jewish speculation about Jesus attributed His conception to a Roman soldier who seduced the young girl Mary.

Thus it becomes clear that while Jesus was growing up in Nazareth the rumors flew. "Mary's son" was the object of nods, winks, and gossip. Her claim—that Jesus had been conceived without a human father—met with the general disbelief that it encounters today.

But Mark from the outset declares Jesus to be "Son of God," and the question still confronts the uneasy conscience of humanity: Who was Jesus of Nazareth? Son of Mary or Son of God?

After the Nazareth disappointment we next find Jesus sending out the twelve. Two marks of a leader are skill in selecting assistants and preparing for the work to continue without him or her. So it was the case with Jesus, leader extraordinaire: He chose wisely and well (only Judas, who thrust himself into the group, didn't pan out), and He trained the apostles by word, example, and on-the-job experience.

The twelve apparently had widespread impact, which would have given Jesus much satisfaction. Immediately after their training mission Mark tells us about Herod's reaction and his comment, perhaps from fear, that "John, the man I beheaded, has been raised from the dead!" (verse 16). Herod Antipas had feared John while he was alive (verse 20). Did bad dreams now haunt the wicked ruler?

So Jesus took the twelve aside to rest, but, as we have seen, the day turned out to be anything but a quiet retreat. It brought the crowds, the apostles, and Jesus face to face with a moment of destiny.

Jesus stood alone, without a single person's support, as He saw the crown of fame and glory dangled before Him. It seemed so easy, as the tempter's offer always does—a shortcut to fulfilling His mission. Satan had offered Him that choice at the outset of the ministry. Now he came again, this time through the cheers, flattery, and eager expectation of a thousand human faces.

Shortcuts can be dangerous. In God's work the end never justifies the means, and means outside the divine will, no matter how attractive or reasonable, corrupt the end.

As He had at the devil's first overture, Jesus once more stood alone.

But not for a moment did He waver or let the tantalizing offer wash around in His mind. Without explanation or equivocation He turned down the crowd and His disciples. Both groups went away unhappy with Him, grumbling and complaining. Then Jesus went up on a mountainside to pray—alone.

Not the path of human glory lay ahead for the Savior. Only the fate of one like Him, the messenger: a grim end at the hands of wicked, cruel, unjust human beings.

6

Mysterious Messiah

(Mark 7:24-9:13)

*J*ust whenever people thought they had Jesus figured out, He surprised—even shocked—them by what He said or did.

And He still does. Because He's too big to fit neatly into the boxes we build for Him, He always breaks out of our theologies and mental packaging.

Throughout the nineteenth century the most brilliant minds of Europe tried to spell out just who Jesus was. Informed by the rationalism of the Enlightenment and casting aside the shackles of church dogma, they devoted themselves to discovering the real Jesus of Nazareth. Out of their intense, century-long endeavor came a series of "Lives" of Jesus that probed the mind and motivation of the Man of Galilee, reconstructing His self-understanding, mission, and death.

How long the scholarly search for Jesus might have continued is anybody's guess, had it not been for a brilliant work that appeared in German in 1906, then later in English. Albert Schweitzer, who earned doctorates in theology, music, and medicine and gave up fame in Germany for a life of missionary service in equatorial Africa, wrote a devastating critique of the "Lives" in his *Quest of the Historical Jesus*. Examining each of the various "Lives," he showed that they were all flawed. Each writer had merely fashioned a Jesus after their own image, be it a German professor or a French scholar.

At the end of Schweitzer's massive book he showed how Jesus eludes analysis and definition. But, argued Schweitzer in a powerful paragraph that closed out the study, we may know who He is, not by scholarly research, but by joining with Him in service.

In Mark 7:24-9:13 we find Peter's ringing affirmation of who Jesus is: "You are the Christ [that is, the Messiah]" (Mark 8:29). The disciple seems to have figured Jesus out, but immediately following his reply we find Jesus sharply rebuking him: "Get behind me, Satan! . . . You do not have in mind the things of God, but the things of men" (verse 34). So Peter, despite his declaration that Jesus was the Messiah, didn't get it. Yes, Jesus was the Messiah, but the mysterious Messiah.

We encounter two strange miracles of Jesus and two puzzling statements in this section of Mark. Some people bring to Him a man who is deaf and has a severe speech impediment and beg Him to put His hand on the individual and heal him. Jesus takes him apart from the crowd, puts His fingers into the man's ears, then spits and touches the man's tongue. Later we meet an even more curious miracle, in which other people lead a blind man to Him. Again Jesus takes the man apart. There He spits on the man's eyes and puts His hands on him. And the man sees again—but not clearly. Only when Jesus puts His hands on him a second time does the person gain his sight fully.

This is strange stuff! What shall we make of it?

The sayings seem equally surprising. To a woman who falls at His feet and begs Him to heal her demon-possessed daughter, Jesus replies: "It is not right to take the children's bread and toss it to their dogs" (Mark 7:27). That sounds cold, harsh, and cruel. After all, who wants to be called a dog? And later He says to the crowd and His disciples: "If anyone would come after me, he must deny himself and take up his cross and follow me" (Mark 8:34). It spells out the path of discipleship, but in terms that have perplexed Jesus' followers from the earliest centuries of Christianity. What can His words mean?

The two strange miracles and two puzzling sayings will provide the framework for our discussion in this chapter. They will, I think, richly reward our attention as we gain fresh insights into Jesus and His ministry. It is when we encounter Him acting or speaking in a surprising or shocking manner that He breaks out of the neatly packaged boxes into which we have put Him.

Before we examine these miracles and sayings, however, we shall look at the travels of Jesus in Mark 7:24-9:13. Noting where He went during this phase of His ministry will give us information about the background to the Bible account, but more important, it will lead us to new insights regarding His mission.

The Journeys of Jesus

We cannot track the travels of Jesus in Mark's Gospel with certainty.

Like the other Gospel writers, Mark does not attempt to present a chronicle of Jesus' ministry. Rather, he presents events and teachings—including some, omitting others—according to the portrait of the Master that, led by the Spirit, he is developing. Thus the journeying of Jesus that we find in Mark 7:24-9:13, while not necessarily giving us a complete picture of His journeys during this period of ministry, provides important insights to what Mark wants to convey.

Jesus first goes to the vicinity of Tyre, a city on the Mediterranean coast (Mark 7:24). Far from Galilee, it is Gentile country. Here He heals the daughter of a Syrophoenician woman.

Then He travels back to Galilee and south to the region of the Decapolis, the Ten Cities (verse 31). It was a large area to the south and east of the Lake of Galilee, with 10 towns that had formed a league for trade and defense about A.D. 1. In addition, it was mainly Gentile in population. In the region Jesus heals a deaf man with a speech impediment.

The next place Mark mentions is Dalmanutha (Mark 8:10), a site as yet unidentified. However, Matthew's parallel account reads "Magadan" (Matt. 15:39), which suggests the town of Magdala on the western shore of Lake Galilee (Mary of Magdala—the Magdalene—came from here). Since Mark tells us Jesus came to Dalmanutha by boat (Mark 8:10), the miracle of feeding the 4,000 that He had just performed probably took place in the Decapolis.

Mark further mentions Bethsaida (verse 22), a town at the northern end of Lake Galilee and home of Peter, Andrew, and Philip (John 1:44). Next the biblical writer refers to Caesarea Philippi (Mark 8:27). Also located near the northern shores of the lake, the city had been named for both the emperor Tiberius and Herod Philip, Antipas' brother, who enlarged and beautified it and ruled over it. Its population was largely non-Jewish during Jesus' time.

As we look at Jesus' journeying, a striking fact emerges: almost all the action takes place in a Gentile setting. Jesus has extended His ministry beyond the chosen people. His mission embraces all people.

From our perspective it seems obvious. Christianity has spread far beyond the confines of Israel, with Jesus confessed as Savior and Lord by far more non-Jews than Jews. But it wasn't evident at the beginnings of the church. All the apostles came out of a Jewish background, and Jesus, Himself a Jew, ministered primarily among His native people. All the early converts after Jesus' death came from Judaism, and Christians continued to go to the Temple and the synagogues. Christianity functioned as a sect within Judaism.

In fact, several years elapsed before the apostles realized that the Lord had given them a *world* mission. Throughout the first nine chapters of Acts we find them preaching—but only to Jews. Then in chapter 10 God blasts through their tunnel vision: He gives Peter a vision and sends him to the centurion Cornelius. And then the Lord raises up Saul of Tarsus, who becomes Paul, apostle preeminent to the Gentiles.

We know that the broadening of the Christian mission caused great tensions in the early church, with Acts 15 recording the first council convened to decide what, if any, of the Jewish ritual regulations the church should require of Gentile converts. No doubt, in this period of earnest searching to know God's will, Christians of all backgrounds would have frequently raised the question of Jesus' teaching and example. At such a time Mark's Gospel would have provided information of great help to them. Earlier, Mark recorded Jesus' debate with the scribes and Pharisees in which He set aside their ceremonial washings (Mark 7:1-23). Now the biblical writer shows how, during His lifetime, Jesus ministered to Gentiles as well as to Jews.

These insights help us to understand some puzzling aspects relating to the feeding of the 4,000 (Mark 8:1-10). Mark's overall account is the shortest of the four, yet he records in detail the two mass feedings. Why go over similar ground with the 4,000 when he had already told the story of the 5,000 (Mark 6:30-44)? And the disciples seem to have quickly forgotten how Jesus fed the 5,000—they don't see how they can help the 4,000. But the issue wasn't whether Jesus could feed the 4,000 (He had demonstrated that ability already), but whether He *would,* since they were Gentiles.

In her classic on the life of Christ, *The Desire of Ages,* Ellen White underscores the point: "Again the disciples revealed their unbelief. At Bethsaida they had seen how, with Christ's blessing, their little store availed for the feeding of the multitude; yet they did not now bring forward their all, trusting His power to multiply it for the hungry crowds. Moreover, those whom He had fed at Bethsaida were Jews; these were Gentiles and heathen. Jewish prejudice was still strong in the hearts of the disciples" (p. 405).

Thus throughout Mark 7 and 8 we find Jesus traveling in areas in which Gentiles predominated. He heals Gentiles and teaches them, and feeds a hungry multitude of Gentiles in just the same manner as He had the 5,000 Jews in Galilee. The conclusion comes home inescapably: Jesus, the Son of God, brings His message and His salvation to all humanity.

With this background we can more readily grasp the meaning behind the two unusual miracles and two sayings we find in this portion of Mark.

Two Strange Miracles

Mark is the only writer to record the healing of the deaf man with a speech impediment and the two-stage restoration of sight of a blind man. Jesus must have performed scores, possibly hundreds, of miraculous healings, but Mark wanted these seemingly odd two to have a place in his record. Why?

Both miracles involve Jesus using spittle in the healing—a detail from the surprising Messiah that many modern readers would be happy to omit. His purpose in doing so eludes our Western-oriented minds, but we may be sure that for the people helped the action had significance in showing His nearness and concern. Anciently people considered the spittle of certain individuals to have healing power, but despite some similarities, Jesus and other wonder-workers differed markedly. His healings did not depend upon a mechanical transfer of power through spittle or any other medium. Furthermore, He did not seek to gain attention or notoriety through them. In both of these strange miracles He took the individual aside and healed in private.

In describing the affliction of the first man, the biblical writer uses a rare word in Mark 7:32, one that indicates that the man had a severe speech defect. The word occurs only here in the New Testament, but we find it in the Septuagint, the Bible that Jesus used, in the messianic prophecy of Isaiah 35: "Then will the eyes of the blind be opened and the ears of the deaf unstopped. Then will the lame leap like a deer, and the mute tongue shout for joy" (verses 5, 6). The prophecy specifically mentions Lebanon, Carmel, and Sharon (verse 2) as seeing the glory of the Lord—that is, the blessing will extend to nations other than Israel.

By placing the healing of the deaf man with the speech impediment in Mark 7:31-37, the Gospel writer, echoing the prophecy of Isaiah 35, further strengthens his presentation of Jesus as the Messiah for all people.

But there is more to this miracle. Mark tells us that Jesus put spittle on the man's tongue, looked up to heaven with a deep sigh, or groan, and said, *"Ephphatha!"*—Aramaic for "Be opened!" Jesus wasn't reluctant to heal the poor individual. Surely He sighed because of those who were sick spiritually but who resisted His saving power. And they included His own disciples, for soon we find a sharp rebuke of the twelve: "Do you still not see or understand? Are your hearts hardened? Do you have eyes but fail to see, and ears but fail to hear?" (Mark 8:17, 18).

And Jesus still sighs over human blindness and deafness. He who touched blind eyes and made them see, and deaf ears and enabled them to hear, could not command men and women in His day to accept Him, nor can He today. He respects human freedom—even the freedom to choose to remain blind to who He is and to remain deaf to His invitation of spiritual healing.

We may understand the second puzzling healing—the blind man whose sight Jesus restores in two stages—along the same lines. At the first stage the man saw again, but with the myopic vision that blurs shapes. Only after the second touch of Jesus' hands did he see everything clearly.

Immediately after the account of this miracle Mark relates Peter's "great confession" at Caesarea Philippi: "You are the Christ [Messiah]" (verse 29). The words were wonderful, inspired by heaven itself (cf. Matt. 16:16), and hearing them, we might conclude that Peter now recognized clearly who Jesus was.

But he didn't. He suffered from spiritual myopia, as did all the disciples, because they thought of Jesus as Messiah in terms that fell far short of God's plan. A Messiah who would suffer, be rejected by the religious authorities, and be killed was not yet in Peter's vision. And the disciple, who had previously given voice to the magnificent confession, soon had the temerity to rebuke Jesus for entertaining such ideas. But it was Peter, not the Lord, who needed correcting, and Jesus didn't mince words: "Get behind me, Satan! . . . You do not have in mind the things of God, but the things of man" (Mark 8:33).

Only afterward—after the cross and the Resurrection—did Peter and His followers see clearly who Jesus was. Years later Peter wrote in a letter to the early Christians: "For you know that it was not with perishable things such as silver or gold that you were redeemed from the empty way of life handed down to you from your forefathers, but with the precious blood of Christ, a lamb without blemish or defect. . . . He himself bore our sins in his body on the tree, so that we might die to sins and live for righteousness; by his wounds you have been healed" (1 Peter 1:18-2:24).

Two Strange Statements

She was a remarkable person, the Syrophoenician woman who wouldn't go away. Jesus had tried to keep secret His presence in the Tyre region, but she found out and immediately went to Him. Falling at His feet, she begged Him to drive the demon out of her daughter.

Jesus didn't answer a word (see Matt. 15:23). But she wouldn't go away.

The disciples discouraged her, wanted to send her off, even urged Jesus to get rid of her (see verse 23). But she wouldn't leave.

Then Jesus spoke—and the words fell like ice on her ears. "First let the children eat all they want," He said, "for it is not right to take the children's bread and toss it to their dogs" (Mark 7:27).

Dogs! How harsh Jesus' reply sounded, especially when we remember that most people in His time considered dogs as nothing more than scavengers and carrion eaters. It breathes the spirit of racial and religious prejudice manifested in a thousand situations across human history. On one side, the favored ones, the elite, "the children"; on the other, the lesser breed, inferior, benighted, "the dogs." This spirit spawned, and still spawns, hatred, bigotry, persecution, slavery, and murder. When you look on someone as less than fully human, you feel free to treat them like an animal—only worse than any animal you own.

One evening on the ABC evening newscast I caught clips from a grisly exhibition—photographs from that terrible period of lynching in the United States from the 1880s to the early 1900s. In one scene a group of Whites stand on a bridge looking down into the camera's lens. Mostly they are men, but it includes boys and women. They pose for the picture without trace of shame or guilt.

Nearby, the charred body of a Black man swings from a tree.

The next photo clip showed a postcard sent the next day from the scene. "We had a barbecue last night . . . ," it tells matter-of-factly.

Could Jesus have partaken of this spirit? Anciently and today, to call a person a dog is to heap scorn and derision on them. "Watch out for those dogs," Paul warned the Philippians (Phil. 3:2). And in the closing verses of the Bible we read, "Outside [the Holy City] are the dogs" (Rev. 22:15).

Jesus classified the Syrophoenician woman with the dogs, but even then she didn't give up. Such a seemingly heartless rejection should have crushed her, but still she stayed.

The woman's persistence provides us with a clue to Jesus' strange behavior toward her. If we could have been there to observe the expression on His face and to catch the tone of His voice, I think we would immediately grasp what He was up to. His words on the surface sounded harsh and uncompromising, but His face must have shone as He spoke in love. The woman caught on: Jesus, despite what He seemed to be saying, wasn't rejecting her—He was welcoming her.

Remember, this story involves more than Jesus and the woman who wouldn't go away. Matthew's account tells us that the disciples also had a part. They wanted to send her off, urging Jesus to do so. And He said nothing—until the strange saying came from His lips. What was He up to? He was playacting, treating the woman as the disciples would have, in an endeavor to reveal to them their prejudiced hearts, to break through the hateful, prideful spirit that they had imbibed simply by being born and growing up as part of "the chosen."

Jesus' ministry would soon conclude, and He would be gone. The twelve would form the nucleus of a movement that He intended to go far and wide. It would begin in Jerusalem with the chosen people, but would at length burst the confines of Israel and spread to earth's farthest bounds.

Mark did not mention the disciples in his telling of the story of Jesus and the woman who wouldn't go away, but he included them as part of his emphasis in chapters 7 and 8—the mission to the Gentiles.

We come now to the second strange saying of Jesus in this portion of Mark: "Then he called the crowd to him along with his disciples and said: 'If anyone would come after me, he must deny himself and take up his cross and follow me'" (Mark 8:34).

The host of interpretations that Christians have advanced over the years and still present—the sufferings of life, pain, ailments, a difficult marriage or work situation—all fall short of Jesus' meaning. *Jesus' call is far more radical and more demanding!*

Jesus' meaning, in fact, is not difficult to grasp. However, we shrink from it, seeking an easier reading, because we don't like what we hear.

Simply put yourself in the shoes of the twelve and the surrounding crowd (Mark tells us Jesus directed the statement to both groups) as they hear His words. They knew exactly what the Master meant: they were familiar with the sight of condemned prisoners trudging down the road carrying the crossbeam upon which they were to be tied or nailed. The Romans practiced crucifixion as a deterrent to would-be rebels, so they made it a public event for maximum effect.

In Mark 8:34, then, Jesus says plainly: My life will terminate on a cross, and if you want to be My disciple, you must be willing to have your life end the same way.

That this difficult saying points inexorably to death becomes clear from the following verse: "For whoever wants to save his life will lose it, but whoever loses his life for me and for the gospel will save it" (verse 35). There is nothing more radical than Jesus' call!

For about 300 years His followers experienced the reality of this saying. Because Christianity had no legal standing in the Roman Empire, they could be burned at the stake or thrown to wild beasts in the Colosseum simply because of their confession of Jesus. Then the emperor Constantine adopted Christianity, and everything changed. Instead of being part of a persecuted minority, Christians found themselves backed by the power of the state. Now they could build churches and gather openly for worship.

Good times—but not without loss. Now it was easy, even advantageous, to profess Christianity. The religion of Jesus became enmeshed in the politics of state. Christians took up arms to fight for its defense. Material concerns came to the fore. And, of course, the day of the sun, Sunday, became the official day to assemble for worship.

But the call to truly follow the Man of Galilee still comes with radical demand. It still exerts the ultimate claim upon us—our very lives. Do we love Jesus more than life itself? Are we willing to give up anything or everything in order to be true to Him?

That is the call from this mysterious Messiah.

7

Power, Sex, and Money

(Mark 9:14-10:31)

Many years ago I read a book titled *Men of Power*. The author's name has long since gone from me, but I remember well the parade of characters—the generals, the heads of state—that passed through its pages with their grasping for control, their manipulation, ruthlessness, and cruelty. And one man of power in particular.

In 1930s Spain a riot breaks out among the soldiers. They're rebelling against the food prepared for them. As the situation drifts out of control, the camp commandant turns to a man clearly on the upward ladder of power, Major Franco. Franco strides to the mess hall and orders the troops to line up for inspection.

"What's the problem, soldiers?" he barks.

A soldier steps forward, tray in hand. "Look at this food, sir," he replies. "It's not fit for pigs to eat." And as he thrusts the tray forward it bumps Franco, and a few drops of slop spill onto his immaculately pressed uniform.

The soldiers standing nearby gasp and hold their breath.

But Franco seems not to notice. He gives orders, calls for better food. Before long the soldiers are sitting down to a good meal, and the mess hall echoes with Franco's praise. But after the meal they receive the order to line up in ranks on the parade ground.

Dressed in a fresh uniform, Franco walks up and down the ranks. He is looking for a face—the face of the soldier who had soiled his uniform.

Finally he recognizes him.

"Soldier, fall out!"

"You—get your rifle!"

"You—get your rifle!"

"You—get your rifle!"

"Fire!"

A man of power. The power of the gun. The power of personality. The power of pride. Power would take Franco to Spain's highest post, and he would rule as unchallenged dictator for many years.

That book I read many years ago told similar stories about the so-called great leaders of this world. But with all the Napoleons, Charlemagnes, and Francos the author presented, he left out one name, the greatest of all.

Jesus Christ.

He commanded no army, won no laurels on the battlefield. But He has influenced countless millions across the face of the planet and continues to do so. At His word they have gone forward into battle—but not with tanks and mortars, missiles and grenades. In His name and by His power they wage warfare every bit as real, every bit as deadly, as Napoleon's or Franco's battles.

Want a man of power? I give you a champion, the King of kings and Lord of lords, who by gentleness and kindly deeds wins the world to Himself. He did not send angels or humans in front of Him to be cannon fodder for the enemy, but went on ahead of us all, dying the death that was ours on Calvary's tree in order to give us the life that was His.

What does this Man of power tell us about power? Our passage for this chapter will reveal the astounding answer, as well as startling answers in two other areas that still play major roles in the lives of men and women today—sex and money.

For this Man of power is radical—this Messiah is radical.

Radical in words.

Radical in action.

Jesus of Nazareth turns on its head the way the world thinks, talks, and acts. And we who would follow Him today must allow Him to turn ourselves on our heads and to let Him use us to turn the world on its head.

Power

Scholars of primitive religions tell us that the worship of Stone Age peoples centered in *mana,* power. They sought to tap life forces that would cause the crops to grow and the women to bear children. Superstition is really the attempt to manipulate for one's interests and well-being, through supposedly efficacious words, acts, or rituals, the *mana* that lies all around us.

Christianity is about power. "I am not ashamed of the gospel," the apostle Paul said, "for it is the *power of God* unto salvation" (Rom. 1:16, KJV). Here is the power—*God's* power. Not power through politicking and scheming or through vaulting ambition and single-minded ruthlessness. Our need is not human power, but *God's* power.

Human power, in fact, gets in the way of divine power. The paradox of Christianity lies in this cosmic truth: "My grace is sufficient for you, for My strength is made perfect in weakness" (2 Cor. 12:9, NKJV), And from the human side: "When I am weak, then I am strong" (verse 10).

Heaven's doors open to the soul that feels and acknowledges its powerlessness. In the Sermon on the Mount Jesus said: "Blessed are the poor in spirit, for theirs is the kingdom of heaven" (Matt. 5:3). Without distorting the text we could paraphrase it: "Blessed are those who aren't hungry for power, for theirs is the kingdom of heaven." Ellen White put it well in a quotation that is one of my favorites: "To him who is content to receive without deserving, who feels that he can never recompense such love, who lays all doubt and unbelief aside, and comes as a little child to the feet of Jesus, all the treasures of eternal love are a free, everlasting gift" (*Signs of the Times,* Feb. 28, 1906).

His disciples were slow to learn this truth, just as we are today. In Mark 9 we find them arguing as they walked along—about who was the greatest! Oh, how blind! When they had the greatest in their midst, how could they look away from Him and stoop to comparing themselves with each other?

Jesus took the twelve apart and sat them down. "If anyone wants to be first," He said, "he must be the very last, and the servant of all" (Mark 9:35). Then He selected a child, had him stand among them, and took him in His arms. "Whoever welcomes one of these little children in my name welcomes me," He said, "and whoever welcomes me does not welcome me but the one who sent me" (verse 37).

The Master identified with the powerless. Here He did so with a child—surely the most powerless element in society during His life on earth. Elsewhere He equated Himself with those who were blind, or deaf, or paralyzed, or disabled; with women, considered second-class citizens; with lepers, outcasts from society; with Samaritans and other Gentiles, those outside the pale of the chosen.

By word and by deed Jesus upended the pyramid built by the social order of His day. That pyramid rested on power, as it still does in our times. Human beings strive to rise higher and higher, struggling, sweating, trampling on those below them, clawing their way to the top. But Jesus takes the pyramid and stands it on its head. Instead of rising by trampling others down, instead having of success by standing on the shoulders of the powerless, He bears the weight of the entire world—the world of the powerless—on His shoulders.

In spite of Jesus' crystal-clear teaching about power, the disciples didn't get it. In Mark 10 we find James and John, the sons of Zebedee, asking Him for a favor—the box seats in His kingdom, one on His right and the other on His left. Again He tried to set them, along with the others, straight. "You know that those who are regarded as rulers of the Gentiles lord it over them, and their high officials exercise authority over them," He said. "Not so with you. Instead, whoever wants to become great among you must be your servant, and whoever wants to be first must be slave of all" (verses 42-44).

Then He capped off the discussion with a statement that summarized His mission to a lost earth, one that has become a Christian classic: "For even the Son of Man did not come to be served, but to serve, and to give his life as a ransom for many" (verse 45).

Only, perhaps, when the disciples saw Jesus give His life on Calvary's tree did they begin to understand the radical nature of His teaching about power. Only then did they get it.

Too often the church has set aside His teaching. The ways and practices of the power-hungry world have invaded the church and corrupted it into a political institution marred by intrigue and vainglory. Christians too often today put business before religion, rationalizing that in the dog-eat-dog modern marketplace the teachings of Jesus about power lead only to failure.

But across the centuries and still today men and women take seriously Jesus' words. His living presence transforms their lives: they regard every human being as valuable, as a child of God. Those whom the world ignores or despises they accept. In Jesus' name and by His grace they reach out in loving ministry to the poor, the hungry, the broken, the helpless—the powerless. And they transform the world.

On a trip to the beach—our favorite place for a breakaway—we met Jodi again. It had been years since we first got acquainted with her and her husband, Mike, when we used to rent a beach apartment they owned. Mike and Jodi bought a catamaran and one day took us out sailing.

Then their lives changed without warning. Felled by a stroke, Mike's mind and body no longer worked. He had to be waited on for all his bodily needs. In appearance he looked just the same, but the Mike we had known was gone.

We lost track of the family until, out of the blue, we saw her in church one Sabbath morning. She looked older, but her eyes still glowed with life and energy.

Tentatively we asked about Mike.

"He's still alive. I have him with me at the beach," she said.

"Is he able to walk or help himself at all?"

"No. He stays in bed, except when I get him into a wheelchair in order to move him. He has to be fed through a tube. And he is incontinent."

"Does he recognize you, show any signs that he knows you?"

"No. Sometimes he talks, but what he says is all over the place. The stroke wiped out his brain functions."

"Jodi, how long has it been?"

"About 14 years. Mike was 51 when the stroke hit, and he's coming up on his sixty-fifth birthday. He may live longer than me!"—the latter with a little smile.

I think of Jodi and 14 years of caring for a spouse who doesn't know who she is, who never shows one response of appreciation. And I think of other options that surely were, and are, available to her. But Jodi chose the path of total love, of total service.

The world may applaud Jodi, or it may dismiss her as a fool who has wasted her life to help someone who will never be anything again. Many will shake their heads in disbelief at her. But those who understand Jesus Christ appreciate Jodi and the road she's chosen. Jodi truly walks in Jesus' footsteps, making Him as real to modern people as when He trod Galilee's shores.

Sex

Mark tells us that the Pharisees set a trap for Jesus, asking Him publicly, "Is it lawful for a man to divorce his wife?" The question was loaded politically, because the ruler over Galilee, Herod Antipas, had divorced his wife and married Herodias, wife of his brother Philip.

John the Baptist had come to grief over this very matter. The fearless preacher of repentance had not minced his words, condemning the marriage of Antipas and Herodias, the latter who had divorced her husband to marry Antipas. It was a public scandal that incensed the people, but John paid with his life for voicing what everyone was saying in private.

Now the Pharisees were trying to snare Jesus. If Jesus replied: "Sure, divorce is OK," He would run against public sentiment. But if He said—as they probably hoped He would—"This marriage is a disgrace and abomination," word would get back to Antipas, who soon would put Jesus behind bars.

Jesus, however, didn't give a yes-or-no reply. Instead He took the discussion back to first principles, and in so doing cast the Pharisees' question in radically new light.

"The question put to Jesus in the passage before us must be set in its ancient context to be appreciated fully. In ancient Judaism, divorce was a right only for husbands; women were legally the property of their husbands and had no power to end the marriage. Further, there was never any question about whether a man might be free to end his marriage by divorce, the only concern reflected in the ancient rabbinic tradition being that a man give proper official certification of the divorce to his wife. There was a difference of opinion between two major schools of ancient rabbinic thought about what were the legitimate causes for divorcing a woman, one school insisting that the only valid reason was sexual impurity in the wife, and the other arguing that the wife could be sent away simply if the husband grew tired of her. The latter view was dominant, no doubt because it was more convenient for a husband" (Hurtado, pp. 146, 147).

Note that the playing field wasn't level for men and women. Jewish law and practice put women in the role of chattels, things (not persons) that their husbands could discard at a whim.

Sad to say, in many societies today such a view of women still prevails. And even in the supposedly enlightened culture of the West, with its laws to safeguard women's rights, the practice often falls short. American society at all levels, beginning with Hollywood, casts women in the role of sex objects for lustful males to use and then toss aside.

Jesus, however, would take us back to God's original purpose. He quoted the Creation account (Gen. 1:26, 27), in which God made us in His image, male and female. Together we bear the divine stamp. One gender is not to have lordship over the other, only mutuality and equality. Next Jesus referred to the divine intent for marriage given in Eden: "For this reason a man will leave his father and mother and be united to his wife, and the two will become one flesh" (Mark 10:7, 8; Gen. 2:24). Becoming "one flesh" rules out of court any view that permits a man or a woman to sever the marriage relationship casually.

Under the laws of Moses a Jewish husband could easily divorce his wife without even going to court. But Jesus set aside such provisions, which, He said, were merely an accommodation to fallen human beings. What He called for was a radical approach that seems to have been without precedent in Jewish thought.

In pointing His hearers back to the Edenic ideal of relations between men and women, Jesus went even further. "Anyone who divorces his wife and marries another woman commits adultery *against her*" (that is, *against his wife*), He said (Mark 10:11). Hurtado notes: "This idea is apparently totally unparalleled in ancient Judaism, where adultery was understood only as an offense committed against another man, either by seducing a man's daughter and depriving him of a marriageable girl, or by violating a husband's exclusive sexual rights with his wife" (p. 148).

Thus Jesus underscored the importance of women in marriage. His teaching, radical for first-century Judaism, speaks to our day with no less compelling power. Abused women, battered women, neglected women, discarded women—the litany of crimes against women stretches to lengths that only God knows.

Only Jesus has the answer to the appalling situations of our times. Politicians and social workers try hard, and I applaud their efforts, but the problem, manifested in cruel and abusive acts, ultimately is one of the heart. Only Jesus can change that—but He can, and does, as individuals yield their will to Him and He makes them over in His image.

Money

A man ran up to Jesus and fell on his knees before Him, Mark tells us (verse 17). Matthew and Luke also record the incident, and from their accounts we learn additional details: the individual was young (Matt. 19:20), and he was a ruler or leader (Luke 18:18).

It is a sad story, made all the more poignant because of a detail that we find only in Mark's Gospel: "Jesus looked at him and loved him" (Mark 10:21). So many of His encounters with individuals had happy endings, but this one did not.

We cannot read the story without a stab of pain at what might have been. The young man had so much going for him—energy, enthusiasm, responsibility, reverence, and religious devotion. He might have become a pillar of the early church, might have been inspired by the Lord to write a Gospel or a letter that would find its way into the canon of Scripture.

But it never happened. At Jesus' words—which cut to the quick of his spiritual experience—his "face fell. He went away sad" (verse 22).

What Jesus said seemed too radical for him. It is still radical and too revolutionary for many people today.

Usually we focus on Jesus' instruction to the young man to sell everything he had, give the proceeds to the poor, and follow Jesus. But before this He said something that stopped the young man in his tracks and that pointed to his spiritual poverty.

The young man approached Jesus with a dramatic flourish: He ran up to Him, fell on his knees before Him, and asked, "Good teacher," "what must I do to inherit eternal life?" (verse 17).

But Jesus brushed aside the flowery opening: "Why do you call me good?" "No one is good—except God alone" (verse 18).

It was a rebuke, softly worded but nonetheless a reprimand. Only God is truly good. Was the young man, thinking to praise Jesus, prepared to acknowledge Him as more than man—as God? His flattering words in fact fell far short of the reality of the God-man before whom he knelt.

And Jesus' soft rebuke had additional ramifications. The young man thought as society in his day did, as we too often reason—he divided people into "good" and "bad." For Jesus, however, the distinction was artificial, because *everyone,* whether "good" or "bad," was a lost sheep whom He had come to seek and to rescue. What mattered—and still matters—is not whether one is a Pharisee or a tax collector, a Nicodemus or a Mary Magdalene. All, regardless of social standing, require the grace of God. Jesus spoke of the need of the grace of God and of the kingdom—God's rule. But more than that, He inaugurated the kingdom. In that kingdom we find no "good" or "bad," because we are all "bad." But we all are saved by grace.

Despite all his sterling qualities, the young man was far from the kingdom. People would have called him "good"—no doubt he'd heard that appellation frequently because of his scrupulous attempts to keep the law— and perhaps that framed his opening line to Jesus: "Good teacher . . ."

One good man to another. A good young man to a good teacher. How much he thought he knew—but actually how little!

Jesus, who reads the heart, understood just what it would take to change the man's thinking and bring him into the kingdom, to expose the paucity of all his previous efforts at righteousness so that he could receive God's gift of eternal life. But to obtain the gift he must first give all away.

"One thing you lack [and how big a thing that one was!]," Jesus said. "Go, sell everything you have and give to the poor, and you will have treasure in heaven. Then come, follow me" (verse 21).

The young man had come to the crossroads of life. He looked down an avenue that stretched strange and uncertain into the future, one without the security and privilege that wealth buys, a road brightened by but one element—the presence of Jesus. Then he glanced to the other road, the continuation of what he had known and loved, a path that guaranteed a safe and comfortable life.

Sorrowfully he turned away from Jesus, unable to bring himself to take the step that led to true life.

Let us be clear as to the story's intent. Jesus does not here advocate poverty as an ideal, just as He does not introduce a social program for the redistribution of wealth.

The point is this: the call of Jesus demands our all. He wants our all (be it little or much), or nothing at all.

Having recognized this central idea, however, Jesus' words speak directly to the issue of possessions in the lives of His followers. After the young man went away, He said to the disciples, "How hard it is for the rich to enter the kingdom of God!" (verse 23).

His comment amazed the disciples. The theology of the day taught that acquisition of wealth demonstrated divine favor. On the other hand, the poor had God's curse upon them.

But Jesus, who spoke for and reached out to the poor, the sick, and the marginalized, directly countered this theology, so comforting to the rich, the well, and the wise. He said again: "Children, how hard it is to enter the kingdom of God! It is easier for a camel to go through the eye of a needle than for a rich man to enter the kingdom of God" (verses 24, 25).

Radical words! No wonder church leaders and theologians through the centuries have tried to escape their plain thrust, inventing such fanciful interpretations for the eye of a needle as a gate or hole in the wall of Jerusalem. Today we would argue that riches per se are no problem, but only as they become our god or are used for selfish or evil purposes.

Hear again Jesus' radical words: Riches *themselves* are a problem. The more possessions we accumulate, the more stuff we acquire, the harder it will be to make it into the kingdom.

Christ's words aren't just for the millionaires and billionaires. They are for all of us, especially if we live in the affluent West. Uncomfortable as they are, we have to face them if we would claim to be followers of Jesus.

History, both ancient and modern, testifies to the truth of Jesus' observation. From its inception "the poor, and the maimed, and the halt, and the blind" (Luke 14:21), rather than those who are affluent, have claimed

Christianity. It was so in the first century of the church and is equally so today. Where people feel rich, well fed, and in need of nothing, they most often turn away at the crossroads of life and follow the path of the rich young ruler; but when they are down and out, struggling to survive or seeking a better life, they are most ready to say yes to the call of the Master: "Come to me, all you who are weary and burdened, and I will give you rest" (Matt. 11:28).

In the Old Testament we find the prayer of Jabez: "Oh, that you would bless me and enlarge my territory! Let your hand be with me, and keep me from harm so that I will be free from pain" (1 Chron. 4:10). The little book based on the passage became a runaway best seller and spun off various peripheral products.

So far I'm not aware of anyone drawing attention to Agur's prayer, also in the Old Testament:

> "Two things I ask of you, O Lord;
>> do not refuse me before I die:
> Keep falsehood and lies far from me;
>> give me neither poverty nor riches,
>> but give me only my daily bread.
> Otherwise, I may have too much and disown you
>> and say, 'Who is the Lord?'
> Or I may become poor and steal,
>> and so dishonor the name of my God" (Prov. 30:7-9)

Don't bother to write a book on this prayer. You won't find many takers. Yet it, not Jabez' prayer, runs closer to Jesus' instruction about money and to the prayer He taught us to offer.

Power, sex, money—they form the motivations of men and women in every age. Mystery writers always come back to these motives to murder as they set up their plots and suspects.

The three—power, sex, and money—intertwine and interact. Power leads to sex and money, while sex and money themselves are power.

Power, sex, money—they continue to shape the world, as they have always. But Jesus the radical Messiah upends our thinking about them. His ideas are so different, the life He calls us to so at odds with the current thinking, that we must cross over from this world (while still in it) and come under His rule, become members of His kingdom.

8

Out of Character

(Mark 10:32-11:25)

*I*nevitably, inexorably, the footsteps of Jesus lead to Jerusalem. Hailed by the crowds in Galilee but dogged by religious leaders who suspected Him and sought to do Him harm, the Master knew that the climax of His mission centered in Judea. Jerusalem summoned Him.

In Luke's Gospel we find Jesus telling the disciples: "I must keep going today and tomorrow and the next day—for surely no prophet can die outside Jerusalem!" (Luke 13:33). While Mark's account does not include a similar statement, nevertheless we find three occasions on which Jesus takes the disciples aside and tells them what awaits Him in Jerusalem (Mark 8:31; 9:30, 31; 10:32-34).

With each occasion the instruction becomes more detailed, more specific. The final passage in the series leaves an indelible picture:

"They were on their way up to Jerusalem, with Jesus leading the way, and the disciples were astonished, while those who followed were afraid. Again he took the Twelve aside and told them what was going to happen to him. 'We are going up to Jerusalem,' he said, 'and the Son of Man will be betrayed to the chief priests and teachers of the law. They will condemn him to death and will hand him over to the Gentiles, who will mock him and spit on him, flog him and kill him. Three days later he will rise'" (Mark 10:32-34).

What a portrait of Jesus! His eye is clear, His chin thrust firmly ahead, His back straight. He knows where He is headed—Jerusalem! And He knows what happens there—Jerusalem kills prophets! But He sets His face like flint, just as Isaiah had predicted: "Because the Sovereign Lord helps me, I will not be disgraced. Therefore have I set my face like flint, and I know I will not be put to shame" (Isa. 50:7).

The disciples, however, are filled with foreboding. Their troubled minds go beyond the usual failure to grasp Jesus' meaning. Now they sense that something terrible will happen in Jerusalem.

Down from Galilee they walk, following the valley of the Jordan until they reach Judea. They come to Jericho, some 800 feet below sea level, with the Dead Sea nearby. The road ahead winds steep and up through the mountains. At the top, at its destination, lies Israel's capital, only 22 miles away, but necessitating a climb of more than 3,000 feet.

The book of Psalms contains a series of songs of ascent (Psalms 120-134). Three times each year—at Passover, Pentecost, and Tabernacles—all Jewish males were required to journey to Jerusalem, and they sang these songs as they made their way to the Holy City:

"Jerusalem is built like a city that is closely compacted together. That is where the tribes go up, the tribes of the Lord, to praise the name of the Lord according to the statute given to Israel" (Ps. 122:3, 4).

Today you make the trip by car. Even so, the road is steep and taxing as it winds through dry, brown hills. Occasionally you see the tents of Bedouin with their animals, but no other signs of life. Perhaps halfway up you come across an ancient inn, dating back to the time of Jesus, and re-member His story of the traveler on the lonely road who fell among thieves but was rescued by a passing Samaritan and taken to a roadside inn.

Then, suddenly, you are climbing out of the hills and looking on set-tlements. You see the Holy City laid out just ahead, with the gold of the Dome of the Rock gleaming in the sunlight.

Jesus walked up this road. He did so resolutely, jaw set firm, face like a flint. The disciples followed behind, wondering, whispering among themselves.

From the Mount of Olives, where the road turned down to the city, they looked over Jerusalem. The city wasn't as big as it is now, and the Dome of the Rock wouldn't yet exist for hundreds of years. But it was still a beautiful city, intriguing and fateful. And dominating it was the huge Temple complex, one of the wonders of the ancient world.

Jesus and His disciples probably arrived on a Friday—the Friday before Passover. The seven days that stretched ahead would be decisive for Jesus, for the twelve—and for the world. One week along, on the next Friday, Jesus would hang suspended between earth and sky on a Roman cross.

This final week of Jesus' life will bring His mission to a climax. Like the other Gospel writers, Mark traces its events day by day, devoting space far out of proportion to the rest of the human existence of Jesus. Mark, like Matthew, Luke, and John, wants us to read and reflect on what happened that week. He doesn't want us to be like the twelve, who didn't get it.

The Gospel of Mark gives six of its 16 chapters to this single week. In chapter 11 Mark tells us about the events of Sunday. And those events, filled with interest, contain surprising elements:

Jesus deliberately draws attention to Himself.

He uses force to drive out the merchants and money changers from the Temple.

And He curses a fig tree because He doesn't find fruit on it, so that the fig tree withers.

Is this the same Jesus with whom we became acquainted earlier in Mark's Gospel? How can He act in a manner so out of character with what we know and expect of Him?

The Triumphal Entry

Sunday morning Jesus sends two of His disciples into a village (probably Bethany, or maybe Bethphage) with a strange order: "You'll find a colt tied as you enter it," He says. "Untie it and bring it here. If anyone asks you what you are doing, tell them the Lord needs it and will send it back shortly."

The disciples go and find a colt tied in the street by a doorway. They loose the colt, and when some of the people standing around ask them what they're doing, they answer just what Jesus had told them.

Then, tingling with excitement, they bring the colt to Jesus. After they throw their coats on the animal, Jesus gets on. And they begin to descend the Mount of Olives to Jerusalem.

All four Gospel writers record the incident. It's essentially the same in all four accounts. As they went along, more and more people joined, until a huge crowd followed. People threw their cloaks on the road; others cut branches from trees and palms and spread them in front of Jesus.

Closer and closer they came to Jerusalem, and still the crowds swelled. Those before and behind shouted out: "Hosanna!" (which means, in Hebrew, "Lord, save us, we pray," based on Psalm 118:25).

"'Blessed is he who comes in the name of the Lord!'

"'Blessed is the coming kingdom of our father David!'

"'Hosanna in the highest!'" (Mark 11:9, 10).

For 600 years the Jews had been a subject people. But the prophets had foretold that another great king like David would arise and lead them to victory. And the prophet Zechariah had described just what that day would be like:

> "Rejoice greatly, O Daughter of Zion!
> Shout, Daughter of Jerusalem!
> See, your king comes to you,
> righteous and having salvation,
> gentle and riding on a donkey,
> on a colt, the foal of a donkey. . . .
> He will proclaim peace to the nations.
> His rule will extend from sea to sea
> and from the River [that is, the Euphrates] to
> the ends of the earth" (Zech. 9:9, 10).

We would say today: from Baghdad to Boston, or from Beijing to Buenos Aires.

The most interesting part about this triumphal entry on Palm Sunday was that Jesus set it up. He orchestrated it. All along He had taken a low-key approach, avoiding publicity, dampening enthusiasm.

But on the Sunday before He died He reversed Himself by getting the colt and riding it down the king's way to Jerusalem, by letting the crowd honor Him as king in act and words. He encouraged the popular expectation that He was the long-awaited Messiah, the new Son of David.

Everybody went wild. Men, women, even children. Peter and the disciples? It was the biggest day of their lives.

But the crowd that shouted "Hosanna!" on Palm Sunday would call out "Crucify Him! Crucify Him!" on Friday morning. The disciples who jubilated with the crowd on Sunday would run away with their tails between their legs on Friday. And Peter, who boldly intended to suffer or die with Jesus if need be, would wilt before a servant girl's questions and three times deny that he even knew Him.

But what was going on that Sunday morning? Why did Jesus, who throughout His work in Galilee had made strong efforts to avoid publicity, now suddenly reverse Himself?

Or did He?

I find Ellen White's comment on the Master's actions particularly helpful:

"Never before in His earthly life had Jesus permitted such a demonstration. He clearly foresaw the result. It would bring Him to the cross. But it was His purpose thus publicly to present Himself as the Redeemer. He desired to call attention to the sacrifice that was to crown His mission to a fallen world. While the people were assembling at Jerusalem to celebrate the Passover, He, the antitypical Lamb, by a voluntary act set Himself apart as an oblation. It would be needful for His church in all succeeding ages to make His death for the sins of the world a subject of deep thought and study. Every fact connected with it should be verified beyond a doubt. It was necessary, then, that the eyes of all people should now be directed to Him; the events which preceded His great sacrifice must be such as to call attention to the sacrifice itself. After such a demonstration as that attending His entry into Jerusalem, all eyes would follow His rapid progress to the final scene" (*The Desire of Ages,* p. 571).

The fact is, Jesus *was* the fulfillment of Zechariah's prophecy of the Messiah. He was Israel's true and rightful king, whose rule—one day—will stretch from pole to pole. While He was not the Messiah of popular expectation, He was the Messiah of God's appointment.

By calling for the colt, riding it into Jerusalem, and doing nothing to discourage the celebration of disciples and the crowd, He proclaimed for all to see that He fulfilled the ancient predictions.

In Galilee the situation called for a low-key approach. He tried to dispel notions that He was merely a miracle worker, a traveling exorcist. While He was such things, He was far more—the Son of God—and the sights and sounds of blind people healed, deaf people rejoicing, and multitudes fed from a few loaves and fishes got in the way of His message. Like people today, most of the Galileans couldn't get beyond appearances.

Now on Palm Sunday He had come to the final, fateful week of ministry. He wanted all eyes to focus on what He was about, as Ellen White noted. He also intended to leave no doubt as to who He was. Later, after the climactic events of that Friday and the following Sunday, the disciples and others would go over the scenes point by point. As their eyes opened to His true person and mission, they would also discern how He fulfilled—in a manner totally unexpected from the popular anticipation—the scriptures that prophesied about Him.

The Refiner Comes to His Temple

Jesus' journey to Jerusalem led straight to its heart, the Temple. In this His final week on earth He would defy and throw down the gauntlet to the religious establishment at the locus of its authority. By doing so He would cause an inevitable backlash and seal His doom.

Even after so many centuries the size and scope of the Temple area still impresses the visitor to today's Jerusalem. One can only imagine the way it dominated the Old City and the religious life of the nation. The Temple that Jesus knew—in which He was dedicated as an infant, where at age 12 He met with the teachers of the law, and into which He entered on Palm Sunday—was much larger than Solomon's Temple. Herod the Great replaced and enlarged the Temple built under Zerubbabel when the Jews returned from exile in Babylon, and the work was still going on during Jesus' ministry. Hence the remark by the Jews to Jesus: "It has taken forty-six years to build this temple" (John 2:20).

We cannot be sure when Jesus drove out the merchants and money changers. Matthew's and Luke's accounts suggest it happened on the Sunday evening after the triumphal entry (Matt. 21:12, 13; Luke 19:45, 46), but Mark puts it the following day. Of that Sunday Mark simply tells us: "Jesus entered Jerusalem and went to the temple. He looked around at everything, but since it was already late, he went out to Bethany with the Twelve" (Mark 11:11).

Since Mark gives a graphic description of Jesus' cleansing the Temple the next day, his account more likely presents the correct order of events. Matthew and Luke telescoped the visits of Sunday evening and Monday.

According to Hurtado, "ancient Jewish evidence indicates that there had been markets for the purchase of sacrificial animals on the Mount of Olives overlooking the Temple for some time, under the jurisdiction of the Jewish Council (Sanhedrin). In about A.D. 30 or so, the high priest seems to have authorized the setting up of similar businesses in the Temple precincts, and this is very likely what Jesus was protesting" (p. 174).

Mark's description of Jesus' actions rivets us: "Jesus entered the temple area and began driving out those who were buying and selling there. He overturned the tables of the money changers and the benches of those selling doves, and would not allow anyone to carry merchandise through the temple courts" (verses 15, 16).

Jesus didn't just drive out animals; He expelled the merchants, pushed over tables and sent coins rattling everywhere, and overturned benches. And He physically prevented anyone from carrying goods through the Temple.

Has Jesus become Rambo? What's happened to the shepherd of Isaiah's prophecy?

"He tends his flock like a shepherd:
He gathers the lambs in his arms
and carries them close to his heart;
he gently leads those that have young" (Isa. 40:11).

Jesus fulfilled those words during His ministry in Galilee. But the Scriptures had also predicted another side to the Messiah:

"Then suddenly the Lord you are seeking will come to his temple. . . . But who can endure the day of his coming? Who can stand when he appears? For he will be like a refiner's fire or a launderer's soap. He will sit as a refiner and purifier of silver; he will purify the Levites and refine them like gold and silver" (Mal. 3:1-3).

Jesus didn't act out of character when He threw out merchants and money changers and took charge of traffic in the Temple courts. He was Lord of the Temple. Its services were supposed to point to *Him*. And the religious establishment had defiled the Temple, turning it into "a den of robbers," supplanting true worship by moneygrubbing. It was time for Jesus to don the role of refiner.

What a scene Mark portrays! The Jesus that emerges turns our preconceptions on their head, two of them in particular.

First, the image of "gentle Jesus, meek and mild" simply won't cut it. Here we see a strong Jesus, an angry Jesus, a Jesus who takes over and uses force. It is a portrait of the Master that has found far too small a place in Christian reflection and art, both anciently and still today.

Second, manipulation of spiritual activities for financial benefit infuriates the Master. Jesus and mammon don't mix, never have and never will. What must He feel today when His name gets invoked in the same breath as appeals for money to make the preacher rich? How would He react to bingo, bazaars, and bake sales in our "temples"?

Let's beware of taking Jesus lightly. He is still the refiner who comes to His temple.

Ficus Is Fired

According to Mark's account, Jesus cursed the fig tree on His way from Bethany to Jerusalem (that is, on Monday morning). He was hungry. Apparently He hadn't eaten breakfast. Noticing a leafed-out fig tree in the distance, He understandably looked to find fruit on it. Green figs ordinarily appear in early spring, before the leaves appear. The fruit ripens in June, but this was a tree out of season, since it was only late March or

April. But the fig tree proved to be a disappointment: it had plenty of leaves but no fruit.

"May no one ever eat fruit from you again," Jesus announced (Mark 11:14). Then He went on to Jerusalem and returned to Bethany that evening. As Jesus and the twelve returned to Jerusalem the next morning they saw the fig tree withered down to the roots. Peter, remembering the incident from the morning before, observed: "Rabbi, look! The fig tree you cursed has withered!" (verse 21).

Critics of the Bible point to this event as evidence that Jesus was a human just like us, subject to loss of temper. They see Him acting out of disappointment and pique. However, a careful reading of the incident in the light of its context and Jesus' earlier teachings gives a quite different understanding.

First, we find this story in Matthew's Gospel as well as Mark's (Matt. 21:18-22). Neither writer displays any embarrassment or tries to water it down. They obviously considered it important enough to include in their account.

Second, we must remember that the cursing of the fig tree took place during the Passion Week. Every word and act of Jesus during those days deserves our closest scrutiny. Nothing is superfluous. Everything is freighted with significance. Since the incident did not occur in full view of the crowds (only the disciples witnessed it), clearly Jesus intended that it should teach them a vital lesson.

Third, the cursing of the fig tree is "a prophetic sign-act, familiar to readers of the Old Testament, an action in which a prophet demonstrates symbolically his message (e.g., Isa. 20:1-6; Jer. 13:1-11; 19:1-13; Eze. 4:1-15). Thus, the act is not to be taken simply as a rash act of anger but as a solemn prophetic word pronounced for the benefit of the disciples (and for the readers)" (Hurtado, p. 168).

Fourth, Jesus' act links directly with a short but powerful parable of a barren fig tree that He told earlier during His ministry (Luke 13:6-9). Each year the owner of the vineyard came seeking fruit, only to be disappointed—it had leaves but no fruit. Then he told the gardener to give the fig tree one more year. Then, if it failed to bear fruit, he should cut it down. The fig tree symbolized Israel (see Isa. 5:1-7), and the parable indicated that it was nearing the close of its probation. By the Passion Week the last grains of sand were running out in its hourglass.

"The parable of the fig tree, spoken before Christ's visit to Jerusalem, had a direct connection with the lesson He taught in cursing the fruitless tree. For the barren tree of the parable the gardener pleaded, Let it alone this year, until I shall dig about it and dress it; and if it bear fruit, well; but if not, then after that thou shalt cut it down. Increased care was to be given the unfruitful tree. It was to have every advantage. But if it remained fruitless, nothing could save it from destruction. In the parable the result of the gardener's work was not foretold. It depended upon that people to whom Christ's words were spoken. They were represented by the fruitless tree, and it rested with them to decide their own destiny. Every advantage that Heaven could bestow was given them, but they did not profit by their increased blessings. By Christ's act in cursing the barren fig tree, the result was shown. They had determined their own destruction" (*The Desire of Ages,* p. 584).

Two details from Jesus' cursing the fig tree drive home the lesson that He sought to convey to His disciples. The fact that the tree had leaves but no fruit meant that it would not bear any fruit at all. Mark notes that "it was not the season for figs," so Jesus did not really expect to find ripe figs on it to satisfy His hunger. The tree was a fake, just as Israel's religion had become all show without the fruit of righteousness that the Lord expected of His people.

Mark mentions that by the next morning the fig tree had withered from the roots. Such a rapid loss of life surely was unusual: in the morning, covered with leaves, but by the next morning, dead—totally dead. Thus it points us away from a purely natural event with natural causes to divine judgment that hangs over the nation.

In Mark's telling of the story he places the cleansing of the Temple squarely between the cursing and the sighting of the withered tree. He records no other teaching or act of Jesus apart from the dramatic act in the Temple.

The connection between the prophetic sign-act and the Temple is surely not coincidental. If Israel had failed God, the rot lay at the center of the nation's worship. The Temple had become a hollow show, with scrupulous concern for ritual but in which love of money (on the part of the priests) supplanted love for God. So far from God's plan and will had the Temple services departed, so bankrupt of true spirituality, that those who organized and led them—the priestly class—failed to recognize the Lord of the Temple when He came to His own. And not merely not recognize—they set about to murder Him!

Leaves—abundant leaves—but no fruit here! This tree will never bear fruit! And it will be smitten by the divine hand, withering to the roots.

It's easy, and tempting, to point the finger at others. We can rail against the Jewish leadership of Jesus' time for their blind stubbornness and rejection of the Messiah, for the futility of their elaborate Temple rituals and sacrifices.

But what about us? What about me? What "fruit" does God look for in my life? Am I leaves only—all show? Or am I bearing "figs" to His glory?

q

Messiah Versus the Temple

(Mark 11:27-12:44)

*I*n chapters 11–13 Mark records the final teaching of Jesus. It falls into two parts: Mark 11:27–12:44, which Jesus gave publicly, and Mark 13:1–37, a private communication to Peter, John, James, and Andrew. Since, as we have noticed, the Gospel writer generally focuses on Jesus' actions and shares little of Jesus' teachings, this portion of Mark's account invites our careful and thorough study. In this chapter we shall study the Master's public words, leaving His private discourse to the following chapter.

Throughout Mark 11:27–12:44 we find Jesus teaching against a background of opposition, intrigue, and treachery. One by one the various elements of the religious establishment—the chief priests and elders, the Pharisees, the Sadducees, the scribes—come forward with questions designed to trip Him up. Not inquiries of the honest seeker after God or truth, they originate from hostile minds and hearts, even when couched in flattery.

Jesus meets each encounter with aplomb. He cuts through the cant and hypocrisy to first principles, exposing the motives behind the hostile questions. Throughout He remains in control, never becoming defensive. And not only do His answers skewer the critics who are hoisted on their own petard; He seizes the occasion to introduce new topics that point His hearers—who include others apart from the critics—to His person and mission.

Throughout the public teaching, which probably took place on the last Tuesday of Jesus' earthly life, we find the Temple mentioned as the backdrop. Indeed, Mark continually reminds us of the Temple setting in such a manner as to alert us to the fact that he intends more than incidental significance by it. Note the references:

Mark 11:11—The triumphal entry leads Jesus not just to Jerusalem but to the Temple.
Mark 11:15—Jesus cleanses the Temple.
Mark 11:27—Jesus' final public teaching commences in the Temple.
Mark 12:35—Jesus teaches in the Temple courts.
Mark 12:41—Jesus sits by the Temple treasury.
Mark 13:1 —Jesus leaves the Temple.

What lies behind the Temple references? Messiah has come to His Temple, but He finds it a hostile place, full of plotting bent on His murder. The Temple has become the heart of a religious system gone to seed, in which ritual has banished spirituality, and filthy lucre counts for more than pleasing God. When Messiah comes to His Temple, it isn't just Messiah in His Temple; it is Messiah *versus* the Temple.

We shall trace in order the events of this final, fateful day—the last day of grace for the Temple itself. Mark will mention it only twice again. He notes the testimony of the false witnesses at Jesus' trial: "We heard him say, 'I will destroy this man-made temple and in three days will build another, not made by man'" (Mark 14:58). And then, in a brief statement pregnant with meaning, he describes the end of the old order of which the Temple was the center: "With a loud cry, Jesus breathed his last. The curtain of the temple was torn in two from top to bottom" (Mark 15:37, 38).

Challenged by the Religious Hierarchy

The first group to confront Jesus, perhaps as soon as He arrived— "while Jesus was walking in the temple courts"—comprised the leaders, "the chief priests, the teachers of the law and the elders" (Mark 11:27). Their challenge did not involve the rightness or wrongness of Jesus' actions. They simply appealed to authority.

"'By what authority are you doing these things?' they asked. 'And who gave you authority to do this?'" (verse 28). No doubt they had in mind the events of the day before when Jesus had driven out the merchants and money changers.

The leaders' challenge finds echoes in every age wherever functionaries of a religious system place the system itself above issues of truth and right. We find it as far back as the Old Testament when God called Amos, a shepherd of Tekoa, to go to Samaria and give a message against the calf worship at Bethel. Amaziah the priest of Bethel tried to intimidate the prophet: "Get out, you seer! Go back to the land of Judah. Earn your bread there and do your prophesying there. Don't prophesy anymore at Bethel, because this is the king's sanctuary and the temple of the kingdom" (Amos 7:12, 13).

But Amos wasn't cowed by the effort to put him in his place; nor did Jesus back off. To the question of authority He posed a counterquestion: "I will ask you one question. Answer me, and I will tell you by what authority I am doing these things. John's baptism—was it from heaven, or from men? Tell me!" (Mark 11:29, 30).

It wasn't an evasive response. In the answer to Jesus' question lay the answer to the leaders' question: the One behind both Jesus and John the Baptist was God. Both spoke at divine direction. And Jesus and John were not only messengers of God's will—they were linked in mission, with John the forerunner of the Messiah and Jesus the Messiah Himself. That is why Mark's Gospel begins not with Jesus but with John (Mark 1:2-13).

By Jesus' counterquestion He challenged the religious hierarchy to come clean about their opinion of John. And that put them on the spot. If they affirmed the Baptist's divine calling, they would be forced to acknowledge Jesus, of whom John spoke also. But to deny John publicly—the encounter took place in full view and hearing of others in the Temple courts—would incur the anger of the people, who looked on the Baptist as a prophet.

Of course, the leaders rejected both John and Jesus. Bound up in their robes of self-righteousness and self-importance, they could brook no challenge to their position as the spiritual hierarchy. But to reveal their thinking would be politically incorrect, so they evaded Jesus' question by replying, "We don't know" (Mark 11:33).

Jesus replied: "Neither will I tell you by what authority I am doing these things" (verse 33). In effect: You have your answer. You rejected John, and now you reject Me.

"We don't know." How much more evidence would it take—how many more miracles, how many more words of life—before they would know? There would never be enough to convince them, because they had closed their eyes and shut up their ears to God. Wrapped in robes of their own weaving, they retreated before the truth into the safety of the system.

A Searching Parable
The leaders had confronted Jesus with a challenge. Now He told a

parable in their hearing. Although a crowd was present (Mark 12:12), everyone could discern the thrust of the words: it was a message aimed squarely at the leadership.

Jesus' hearers were familiar with the Song of the Vineyard in the book of Isaiah: "I will sing for the one I love a song about his vineyard: My loved one had a vineyard on a fertile hillside. He dug it up and cleared it of stones and planted it with the choicest vines. He built a watchtower in it and cut out a winepress as well. Then he looked for a crop of good grapes, but it yielded only bad fruit" (Isa. 5:1, 2). Jesus retold the story, giving it a new twist. Whereas in Isaiah the emphasis falls on the failure of the vineyard, representing Israel, to produce fruit, now the locus shifts to the tenants of the vineyard, who do not appear in Isaiah's version.

In Jesus' parable the tenants behave disgracefully. They ill-treat the succession of servants that the owner dispatches to them, beating some, insulting others, even killing several. And the tenants never send any fruit to the owner.

Why do the tenants act so brazenly? Because they fail to recognize their place—that they aren't the owners but merely tenants. They have usurped the rights of the owner.

Jesus' parable cut the religious leaders to the quick. They would have loved to seize Him on the spot, but they were afraid of the crowd. His words struck home, because their attitude to the Temple and to religious affairs mirrored that of the tenants. While failing to produce the fruit of righteousness, they had forgotten that God was the object of the Temple worship and Israel's religion.

His parable rises to a climax. The owner "had one left to send, a son, whom he loved. He sent him last of all, saying, 'They will respect my son'" (Mark 12:6). But the tenants, blind to reality, in their self-absorption did not. Instead they saw the son's arrival as an opportunity to seize the inheritance for themselves.

"So they took him and killed him, and threw him out of the vineyard" (verse 8). Their reaction is incredible, even at the level of story. Our sense of justice rises up in indignation at the wickedness of the tenants. And astonishment at their self-delusion. How could they be so stupid? Did they think they could really get away with murder?

If the tenants' actions amaze and repulse us, what shall we say of the application? What colossal stupidity, what blindness of self-delusion, led to the religious leaders treating the Son of God in the very same way: "They took Him and killed Him, and threw Him of out of the vineyard"?

Jesus spoke these words on Tuesday. Three days later the religious establishment would literally take and kill Him outside the city of Jerusalem.

An Unholy Plot by an Unholy Alliance

The religious leaders went away, but continued to scheme. Next Mark tells us, "They sent some of the Pharisees and Herodians to Jesus to catch him in his words" (verse 13).

Works of darkness make strange bedfellows. Normally the Pharisees and Herodians were poles apart in ideology. But both groups hated Jesus sufficiently to lay aside their differences in a common cause.

They approached Him with words of flattery. "Teacher," they said, "we know you are a man of integrity. You aren't swayed by men, because you pay no attention to who they are; but you teach the way of God in accordance with the truth" (verse 14).

Flowery phrases, but totally insincere, designed so that Jesus would let down His guard and say something they could use against Him. Then the question, so harmlessly couched but loaded: "Is it right to pay taxes to Caesar or not? Should we pay or shouldn't we?" (verses 14, 15).

Either way—however Jesus replied—they had Him. If He said no, the Herodians could hightail it to Pontius Pilate, and Jesus would be in big trouble. But if He said yes, the Pharisees could accuse Him of going along with the hated Roman occupation.

The annual tax levied by Rome especially vexed the Jews. Not only did it demonstrate their subject status, but it had to be paid in Roman money—and the common coin, the denarius, bore the likeness of the emperor with the inscription "Tiberius Caesar, Augustus, Son of Divine Augustus"—that is, as a semi-divine being. Such a claim greatly offended the Jews—it was blasphemous.

Jesus met the seemingly difficult situation in masterly fashion. Cutting through the claptrap, He flung a question back at His enemies: "Why are you trying to trap me?" (verse 15). Then He asked them to hand Him a denarius. He didn't carry the coin with the hated image, but *they* did! So much for their vaunted piety.

Nor would He let them off the hook easily. "Whose portrait is this? And whose inscription?" (verse 16) He asked, holding up the coin, forcing them to reveal their hypocrisy.

"Caesar's," they mumbled, squirming before the crowd.

Then came the classic statement: "Give to Caesar what is Caesar's and to God what is God's" (verse 17). By it Jesus established a legitimate but specific role for the state. He separated Himself from those in His time or any time who use violence or other means to overthrow government and establish a theocracy. But He likewise distanced Himself from any and all efforts to elevate the state to divine claims—as the inscription on the denarius implied.

A Trick Question

One more group of people tried to embarrass Jesus. The Sadducees approached with a stock question and motives every bit as slippery as those of the previous critics.

Since the Sadducees left no writings, our knowledge of them is more limited. Mark informs us that they denied the resurrection (verse 18), and Luke notes that in addition they rejected the existence of angels and spirits (Acts 23:8). The Sadducees were "a minority religio-political Jewish party of New Testament times representing the wealthy, aristocratic, liberal, secular-minded wing of Judaism. . . . They had a strong concern for the secular affairs of the nation, willingly accepted public office, and exerted an influence far beyond that which their numbers would seem to warrant" (*Seventh-day Adventist Bible Dictionary,* p. 943).

The Sadducees accepted only "the Law"—the first five books of the Bible—as inspired. Yet, strange as it seems, they held the high priesthood during the time of Jesus. How far had Jewish spiritual affairs fallen! The leaders of Israel's worship at the Temple were secular individuals whose focus fell on events in this life instead of the hereafter.

Relishing debate with the Pharisees, who affirmed the resurrection, the Sadducees liked to embarrass them with a story from the Apocrypha of the woman who married seven brothers in succession. They now put it to Jesus, not with any intent to learn truth, but to make fun of Him and any belief in an afterlife. The punch line seemed to make their argument unassailable: "At the resurrection whose wife will she be, since the seven were married to her?" (verse 23).

But Jesus didn't squirm. Instead He replied: "Are you not in error because you do not know the Scriptures or the power of God? When the dead rise, they will neither marry nor be given in marriage; they will be like the angels in heaven" (verses 24, 25). Then He quoted Exodus 3:6, in which the Lord calls Himself the God of Abraham, the God of Isaac, and the God of Jacob, as biblical proof that the dead will rise.

In several books of the Old Testament, notably Job, the Psalms, Isaiah, and Ezekiel, we find allusions to the resurrection. However, the

Sadducees did not accept the inspiration of such books, hence Jesus quoted from the portion that they did accept, the Law, or Pentateuch. By doing so He called upon a biblical proof that, so far as is known, the Pharisees had never discerned.

In Luke's account of the same incident we find these additional words: "He is not the God of the dead, but of the living, *for to him all are alive*" (Luke 20:38). That is, although Abraham, Isaac, and Jacob—and indeed, all the righteous ones of the ages—die and rest in the grave, they are bound up in the life of God. And that life inevitably shall call them forth from the tomb at God's appointed time.

So, Jesus said, the Sadducees really didn't understand the very Scriptures in which they took pride, nor did they know God's power— His ability to change the present world order of marriages, births, and deaths. The Sadducees had made this life the measuring stick of the future, but in doing so had neglected God. How true this still is!

Concerning the future world order, Ellen White wrote: "There are men today who express their belief that there will be marriages and births in the new earth, but those who believe the Scriptures cannot accept such doctrines. The doctrine that children will be born in the new earth is not a part of the 'sure word of prophecy.' The words of Christ are too plain to be misunderstood. They should forever settle the question of marriages and births in the new earth. Neither those who shall be raised from the dead, nor those who shall be translated without seeing death, will marry or be given in marriage. They will be as the angels of God, members of the royal family" (*Medical Ministry,* pp. 99, 100).

A Sincere Question

The day was wearing away, but Jesus received yet another question. It came from a "scribe," and unlike the previous ones it arose from a true heart. "You are not far from the kingdom of God," Jesus said to the inquirer at the close of the conversation (verse 34).

The person who posed this question was a teacher of the law. Members of the group devoted themselves to the study of the Scriptures and had high respect for their learning. "Scribes wore white linen robes reaching to their feet as a sign of their devotion to the Law and their special place in Jewish life, and upon their approach other Jews would stand to show their respect and greet the scribe with titles of honor like 'master' or 'father.' At banquets a scribe would often be given a special place of honor and recognized publicly. In synagogues the scribe would be offered a seat at the front facing the congregation" (Hurtado, p. 193).

We might conclude that a life devoted to the study of the Word would result in godliness, but it does not necessarily follow. True, the Word has power to transform, but only if the heart is open to the divine influence. When people study the Bible primarily to acquire knowledge, they can become learned teachers far from the kingdom of God. And the acclaim that one receives from others closes the heart even more tightly against God's will. Thus it was in Jesus' day and thus it still is. Some of the leading scholars of the Bible today may make no profession of following Jesus Christ, the Lord of the Word.

In Mark and the other Gospels, therefore, we find the scribes as a class united with those who oppose Jesus and eventually want Him out of the way. He directed some of His sharpest criticisms against the "scribes and Pharisees, hypocrites!" (see Matt. 23, especially verses 13, 15, 23, 25, 27, 29). And here, as His last day of public teaching drew to a close, Jesus said: "Watch out for the teachers of the law. They like to walk around in flowing robes and be greeted in the marketplaces, and have the most important seats in the synagogues and the places of honor at banquets. They devour widows' houses and for a show make lengthy prayers. Such men will be punished most severely" (Mark 12:38-40).

While Jesus condemned the scribes as a class, He did not dismiss them out of hand. His ear was open to any individual, regardless of what group they might belong to, who was ready to listen to Him. And so when one of the teachers of the law raised a sincere question, Jesus commended him for his honest search to know and follow God's will.

The scribe's question raised a matter that the Jews frequently discussed: "Of all the commandments, which is the most important?" (verse 28). The Jews counted 613 commandments in the Torah and understandably looked for an organizing principle or center for all of them.

Mark tells us that the scribe in question had been listening intently to Jesus' debate with the Sadducees. Noting that Jesus "had given them a good answer," he decided to raise the longstanding question as to the heart of the law—not to try to trap Him but out of a sincere desire to hear His response.

Jesus replied by quoting two passages from the Torah. He designated the first one He cited, which we find in Deuteronomy 6:4, 5, as "the most important": "Hear, O Israel: The Lord our God, the Lord is one. Love the Lord your God with all your heart and with all your soul and with all your strength." Then He quoted Leviticus 19:18: "Love your neighbor as yourself."

So the center of the law is in the heart. As with all of the 613 commandments, the law ultimately reaches beyond what we can reduce to rules, for love cannot be spelled out. It was the same point Jesus elaborated in the Sermon on the Mount when He called for a righteousness that surpasses that of the Pharisees and scribes (Matt. 5:20).

The final comment by Jesus in His encounter with the teacher of the law leaves us wondering. "You are not far from the kingdom of God," the Master commended him. But "not far" is still outside. Did the scribe eventually open his heart all the way and become a follower of Jesus? How I would like to know!

Mark now tells us: "And from then on no one dared ask him any more questions" (Mark 12:34). Jesus had silenced them all—priests, elders, Pharisees, Sadducees, Herodians, scribes.

But there still remained one final question to close off the day. With this one, however, Jesus would turn the tables.

The Final Question

Jesus asked the last question. Through it He challenged the scribes as "the large crowd listened to him with delight" (verse 37). But His query involved far more than matters of interpretation: it was the ultimate question—for the scribes, for the crowd, and for us today.

"How is it that the teachers of the law say that the Christ [Messiah] is the son of David?" He asked. "David himself, speaking by the Holy Spirit, declared: 'The Lord said to my Lord: "Sit at my right hand until I put your enemies under your feet."' David himself calls him 'Lord.' How then can he be his son?" (verses 35-37).

Jesus here quoted Psalm 110:1. The writers of the New Testament refer to the short psalm more than any portion of the Old Testament, with the book of Hebrews continually playing on verse 4: "You are a priest forever, in the order of Melchizedek." If that verse challenged the Israelite priestly order founded on Aaron, the first verse called into question the current thinking about the identity of the Messiah.

The Jews looked back to David as the ruler par excellence—he who defeated enemies on every side and reigned with justice and equity. After they lost their independence they continued to hope for the "Son of David"—a new king coming in David's line who would recapitulate the golden era. He would be the Christ, the Anointed One, who would lead Israel's armies to victory against the hated Romans.

But Jesus, by probing Psalm 110:1, showed that it wasn't sufficient merely to call Messiah the Son of David. The Messiah would be more than David's descendant: He would be his Lord, one far greater than the ancient Israelite king.

Through this discussion Jesus pointed to a more important subtext, specifically the issue of who He Himself was. For years rumors and whispers about the preacher-healer from Galilee had stirred the people: Could the long-awaited Messiah have come? And just a couple days before, Jesus had ridden into Jerusalem in triumph with the crowd hailing Him as Messiah.

Now He in effect confronts the scribes and the crowd: You say I am the Messiah, but do you realize who Messiah will be? Not just the Son of David, but Lord of David!

Here we have the incident at Caesarea Philippi replayed. "Who do people say that I am? . . . But who do *you* say that I am?"

It was Jesus' final question because it is the ultimate one, haunting men and women of every age and refusing to go away. Because Jesus is the man who won't go away. Reject Him we may, spit on His face, turn our backs on Him—but He is still *there*.

For John Mark, who wrote this Gospel, and for all the New Testament Christians, the answer calls for a life-changing decision. It is a response built on a basis of fact but transcending fact and becoming faith: "Jesus Christ [is] the Son of God" (Mark 1:1).

A Gift of Love

The Master had had a long and trying day. Conservative critics, liberal critics, political critics—all had sought to embarrass Him before the crowds in the Temple or to garner material that they could use against Him in court. But Jesus had deflected each thrust with grace and Scripture-laced skill. Now, as He was about to leave the Temple for the last time, He encountered someone at the lowest rung of the social order but who ranked high on heaven's list.

As He sat by the Temple treasury and watched the crowd putting in their money, He noticed a poor widow, trying not to be seen, drop in two lepta—two copper coins, the smallest in circulation, worth less than a penny in today's currency. The widow quickly slipped away unnoticed and unappreciated by all—except Jesus.

"Calling his disciples to him, Jesus said, 'I tell you the truth, this poor widow has put more into the treasury than all the others. They all gave out of their wealth; but she, out of her poverty, put in everything—all she had to live on'" (Mark 12:43, 44).

Commentators and preachers customarily focus on the smallness of the widow's gift, but Jesus regarded it in just the opposite terms. For Him, it was a magnificent gift, a huge and sacrificial one. Not how little—but how much!

When Bill Gates presents $1 billion to a charitable foundation, the media takes notice. They comment on the size of the gift, and, I suppose, rightly so. But if Bill Gates gives $1 billion or $10 billion or $20 billion, he still has billions left. You can eat a long time on just $1 billion.

After the widow dropped in the two lepta, she had nothing—nothing!—left. Nothing in the bank. No credit cards. No stash of cash under the bed. She gave her last money, little as it was, big as it was.

And nobody noticed that her gift was greater than Bill Gates's $1 billion.

Nobody—except Jesus.

He noticed.

And He still notices.

10

On Guard

(Mark 13:1-37)

*I*n Mark 13 we come to the final teachings of Jesus. Not His last earthly words—He will utter them as He hangs on the cross—but His concluding block of instruction. And a person's last remarks warrant our close attention.

When someone is dying, relatives and close friends gather by the bedside. They hang upon the person's every word, gathering and storing them in memory's jewel box to take out and lovingly handle again and again in the days and years that follow. Only those who *belong*—who have close ties of blood or affection—are welcome at the bedside vigil. It is a *private* gathering, and the last treasures are intended for private use.

Throughout the Old Testament we find final remarks singled out for emphasis. As Jacob was dying he called for his sons to gather around, and then pronounced his prophetic blessing on each (Gen. 49:1-28). Moses, told by the Lord that he must shortly die on Mount Nebo, blessed the 12 tribes (Deut. 32:48-33:29). Joshua, feeling the icy breath of death on his neck, summoned the leaders of Israel for a final message (Joshua 23:1-24:30). And Scripture also records King David's last words and charge to his heir Solomon (2 Sam. 23:1-7; 1 Kings 2:1-11).

All four Gospel writers tell us that, just prior to the events that led to Jesus' crucifixion, He spent time with those who were closest to Him, His friends the disciples. Throughout His ministry His words went out to all who chose to listen. During the first few days of the Passion Week He maintained a highly public presence as He disputed in the Temple with Pharisees, Sadducees, scribes, and Herodians. But now, with the shadow of the cross casting its pall, He gave a private discourse to the twelve.

He didn't intend His words for a general audience. Only those who belonged, who loved Him and whom He loved so dearly, qualified to receive this discourse. Jesus wanted to speak to them about the days ahead—when they would be on their own. The Master sought to prepare them for a new and at times dangerous future.

Are you a friend of Jesus? He meant His last words especially for you. You belong in the circle!

While Matthew, Mark, Luke, and John all record Jesus' final, private discourse with His friends, John's account varies considerably. Matthew 24, Mark 13, and Luke 21, however, cover the same ground. Mark reports that Jesus sat on the Mount of Olives opposite the Temple and told Peter, James, John, and Andrew what they could expect after He had left them.

His remarks sprang from an exchange that occurred as they walked out of the Temple for the final time on that Tuesday (possibly Wednesday) evening. One of the disciples, noticing the huge foundations of the superb structure (consisting of blocks more than 25' x 8'), commented: "Look, Teacher! What massive stones! What magnificent buildings!" (Mark 13:1).

But Jesus replied, "Do you see all these great buildings?" "Not one stone here will be left on another; every one will be thrown down" (verse 2).

Imagine the consternation of the disciples. Such a calamitous event must surely mean the end of all things. So a little while later, as they sat on the Mount of Olives with the sun's last rays gleaming from the gold leaf and white marble of the Temple opposite them, they asked Jesus: "Tell us, when will these things happen? And what will be the sign that they are all about to be fulfilled?" (verse 4).

And Jesus opened up a window on the future, foretelling not merely the destruction of the Temple but also the end of the age when He will return.

John, however, in his account passes by all this material, apparently concluding that the other writers have covered it fully. Instead, he focuses on Jesus' last moments with the twelve, on the Thursday night just before His capture. In a long discourse that also deals with the future (John 13-17) Jesus comforts His friends and promises that He will continue to be with them through the coming of the Paraclete, the Holy Spirit. In Mark 13 we learn of events in the world, while in John 13-17 we hear of the life of the disciples after Jesus has left our earth.

His final words—the discourse we find in the Synoptic Gospels and that in John's account—contain precious instruction. They are Jesus' parting legacy to us, His friends, we who belong at His side.

Apocalypse: The End Is Near!

Mark 13, like Matthew 24 and Luke 21, comprises apocalyptic material. The word comes from the Greek *apokalupsis,* which occurs first in Revelation 1:1—"The *revelation [apokalupsis]* of Jesus Christ, which God gave him to show his servants what must soon take place."

Thus the root meaning of *apocalypse* is an unveiling, a revealing of the future. The entire book of Revelation, called by many the Apocalypse, deals with what will take place in the future, but Revelation is not the only book of apocalyptic in the Bible. Long before it the book of Daniel sketched the future in ways that Revelation echoes and elaborates. But unlike Daniel, which contains several narrative chapters, Revelation consists wholly of apocalyptic material.

While Daniel and Revelation furnish the clearest examples of apocalyptic writings, we find chapters here and there elsewhere in Scripture that reflect its characteristics—for example, Isaiah 24, Joel 2, and Zechariah 14 in the Old Testament. In the New we have 1 Thessalonians 4 and 2 Thessalonians 2. Apocalyptic is a particular form of biblical prophecy that prominently features the end of the world.

As we have already learned from Mark 13, apocalyptic is private discourse, divine instruction for God's people who face an uncertain future. It's meant to give them insight into what lies ahead and assurance that the Lord is with them and will bring all things to a happy conclusion. So we find scattered throughout apocalyptic hints and suggestions that God did not intend such material for a general audience but for those close to God who will read and understand. "But you, Daniel, close up and seal the words of the scroll until the time of the end. Many will go here and there to increase knowledge" (Dan. 12:4). "He who has an ear, let him hear what the Spirit says to the churches" (Rev. 2:7, 11, 17, 29; 3:6, 13, 22). "This calls for wisdom. If anyone has insight, let him calculate the number of the beast" (Rev. 13:18).

In apocalyptic writings the revelation of the future often comes encoded in symbols. Daniel saw a vision of a great image (Dan. 2); King Nebuchadnezzar dreamed of a tree suddenly cut down (Dan. 4); a bloodless hand wrote mysterious words on the palace wall (Dan. 5); and first in a dream (Dan. 7) and then in a vision (Dan. 8) the prophet beheld a series of beasts that represented the rise and fall of nations. In Revelation the future unfolds through a series of vivid scenes, both in heaven and on earth, with the forces of evil portrayed as fantastic, rapacious beasts, and the forces of good marshaled as armies under the banner of Jesus

Christ, whose most common title in the book is "the Lamb."

The Bible is not the only place in which one can find apocalyptic writings. In the centuries just before Jesus the Jews produced a series of apocalypses such as 2 Esdras and the Psalms of Solomon, while a little later some Christians apart from John the revelator wrote apocalypses that the earthly church did not consider inspired and left out of the canon of Scripture (e.g., the Shepherd of Hermas).

During the past two millennia of Christian history the church largely neglected the apocalyptic writings of Scripture. As it settled down with the conversion of the Roman emperor Constantine, the focus shifted from a coming kingdom of God to one right here and now. As church and state combined, the millennium would in due course result on this earth. Eventually, of course, that dream collapsed. With the Enlightenment of the seventeenth and eighteenth centuries religion found itself on the run before the advance of reason. Knowledge and education would solve the problems of society as humanity, which had evolved from the slime, would continue to improve. No need for divine intervention such as the second coming of Christ and the end of the world. Apocalyptic was for pessimists and ignoramuses.

Into such a milieu—the unbridled optimism about the inevitability of human progress—the Seventh-day Adventist movement was born. With our revival of study of long-neglected biblical apocalyptic, especially the prophecies of Daniel and Revelation, and our message that time was running out for the world, we seemed to be doomsayers, a crazy voice in the wilderness. But we painted our convictions right into our name—Seventh-day *Adventists*—and flung them in the face of a scoffing society.

How times have changed! The rosy future of the early twentieth century crashed in flames as World War I—a conflict between supposedly Christian nations—engulfed humanity in a global nightmare. And that was only the beginning of a violent, bloody century that became embroiled in hatred, torture, unspeakable cruelty, violence, and fear. We learned to live with the threat of global annihilation as atomic weapons hung over our heads. Now, to add to that danger we find ourselves in the midst of global terrorism and new threats from chemical and biological weapons.

Our language has changed. *Apocalypse* has become a household word. But it isn't the apocalypse of John and the other Bible writers, in which Jesus reveals the future to His friends and gives them assurance and encouragement for the hard times ahead. Rather, today apocalypse means that the end is coming—through war, an asteroid impact, or an invasion from outer space. It is apocalypse without Jesus, without hope.

At such a time as this the Adventist message has never been more relevant. It offers hope, comfort, and assurance that Jesus is in control. That *He,* not warmongers or asteroids or aliens, will ring down the curtain on human history. And that we can put our hand in His—the hand that was nailed to the cross for us—and He will never let us go.

That's the message of Mark 13.

Interpreting Mark 13

Unlike the books of Daniel and Revelation, Mark does not feature symbols, beasts, and calculations. In just one place Jesus refers to Daniel: "When you see 'the abomination that causes desolation' standing where it does not belong . . . then let those who are in Judea flee to the mountains" (verse 14; cf. Dan. 9:27; 11:31; 12:11). His prediction found fulfillment in the invasion of Israel by imperial Rome, when Titus captured Jerusalem and destroyed the Temple in A.D. 70.

Throughout Mark 13 the emphasis falls on the need for Jesus' followers to be on guard against deception and dangers of various kinds:

"Watch out that no one deceives you" (verse 5).

"Many will come in my name, claiming, 'I am he,' and will deceive many" (verse 6).

"You must be on your guard. You will be handed over to the local councils" (verse 9).

"If anyone says to you, 'Look, here is the Christ!' or, 'Look, there he is!' do not believe it" (verse 21).

"False Christs and false prophets will appear and perform signs and miracles to deceive the elect—if that were possible" (verse 22).

"So be on your guard; I have told you everything ahead of time" (verse 23).

"Be on guard! Be alert! You do not know when that time will come" (verse 33).

"Therefore keep watch" (verse 35).

"What I say to you, I say to everyone: 'Watch!'" (verse 37).

Thus the theme of Mark 13, sounded again and again, is *alertness.* As we wait for Jesus to return, we must stay awake, keep ready for action, and stand at our post. The time between Jesus' ascension and second coming will pose three types of dangers for His followers: first, false christs and false prophets, performing signs and miracles, who lead people into thinking that the end has already come; second, persecution, hatred, and difficulty that cause faith to waver, especially when family and friends turn their backs and betray; and finally, a gradual loss of anticipation of Jesus' return so that His coming takes us by surprise.

As Jesus sat with Peter, James, John, and Andrew on the Mount of Olives that evening, He looked across the sweep of human history to the end of time. That He clearly intended to cover the period ending in His second advent we see in a specific reference to that event: "At that time men will see the Son of Man coming in clouds with great power and glory. And he will send his angels and gather his elect from the four winds, from the ends of the earth to the ends of the heavens" (verses 26, 27). Likewise Mark 13 contains numerous references to "the end" and expectations of it (verses 7, 8, 10, 13, 29, 32, 35).

The disciples' question, however, dealt with the destruction of the Temple. Jesus' comment that the day would come when not one stone would remain upon another must have stunned them. They wanted to know more. "Tell us," they asked Him, "when will these things happen? And what will be the sign that they are about to be fulfilled?" (verse 4).

Jesus' preview of the future from the Mount of Olives thus covers two concerns: the signs of the fall of Jerusalem and those of the end of the world. To the disciples with their foreshortened view of history, the events were coterminous—the end of the Temple must surely signify the close of human history on the planet. Matthew's account of their question makes this clear: "'Tell us,' they said, 'when will this happen, and what will be the sign of your coming and of the end of the age?'" (Matt. 24:3).

In interpreting Mark 13, therefore, we need to keep in view the double foci of the passage. Some verses relate primarily to the fall of Jerusalem and the destruction of the Temple in A.D. 70, while others clearly designate events leading up to the Second Coming. Several verses leave us in doubt as to the schema in which they best fit. Possibly they apply in both the first century and later.

While we cannot claim an exact analysis of the chapter, the following outline seems persuasive:

An overview of the future (verses 5-8).

    1. deceptions (false christs, false prophets)

    2. wars

    3. rumors of wars

    4. national and international conflicts

    5. earthquakes

    6. famines

Living in troubled times (verses 9-13).
1. Christ's followers arrested and flogged
2. witnessing before governors and kings
3. the gospel preached to all nations, despite the persecution
4. the Holy Spirit supplying words when we find ourselves put on trial

Signs of the impending fall of Jerusalem (verses 14-23).
1. the "abomination of desolation" (Roman armies) entering the Temple
2. necessity for rapid flight from Jerusalem
3. days of distress
4. false christs and false prophets
5. signs and miracles of great power to deceive

Signs of the end of the world (verses 24-29)
1. sun darkened
2. moon not giving light
3. the stars falling
4. heavenly bodies shaken
5. the Son of Man coming with great power and glory
6. a lesson from the fig tree

The critical quality: Watch! (verses 30-37)
1. this generation to see it
2. Christ's words never to pass away
3. the day and hour unknown
4. a lesson from the householder who goes away
5. ready at all times to meet the Master

We could wish for a neatly ordered series, listing events and signs extending from that evening on the Mount of Olives through the fall of Jerusalem, across the long ages, and culminating in the return of Christ. But Jesus didn't set out to give a lesson in "history in advance." He wanted to provide *spiritual preparation* for His friends, as they would face an uncertain future. And God in His wisdom knows best. We probably would misuse a list of signs and events that told us just when to expect the Second Coming. A lot of us would put off the needed preparation until the last minute.

What we have, then, isn't a chart of the future that provides us with superior knowledge in which we can take pride. (Who wouldn't love to have such a chart!) Rather, we have a spiritual road map good for any time and place between now and the Second Advent. As we hear of wars and rumors of wars; as false christs and false prophets arise—even working miracles; as nations and superpowers threaten and clash; as earthquakes strike with increasing frequency and severity; as famine stalks large areas of the world; as God's people suffer abuse, false arrest, flogging, imprisonment, and death itself; and as the gospel message goes onward and forward to earth's remotest bounds—with all these events, *in* all these events, we know that He is near, even at the door. Observing the fig tree teaches us that summer is about to burst over the world.

In light of this analysis of Mark 13 we may better grasp a verse that long has puzzled students of the Scriptures: "I tell you the truth, this generation will certainly not pass away until all these things have happened" (verse 30). Some Adventists have understood Jesus here to say that the generation that sees the signs in the heavens—sun darkened, moon darkened, stars falling—will live to see His return. For a time they could cling ever more tenuously to that interpretation, but now no more. Far too many years have passed. That generation is long since dead and buried.

Did Christ's words fail? Not at all. The answer lies in the double foci of the chapter. "This generation" applies, not to the time before the Second Coming, but to the disciples' era. Surely *"this* generation" designates their generation. And Jesus is warning them: "Listen! The destruction of the Temple is near at hand. People now living will witness it."

Immediately following He makes the prediction that His words will never pass away. The time reference here seems long, far beyond the fall of Jerusalem. Thus the two foci of the chapter abut each other as Jesus finishes His discussion of the "signs" and concludes with the exhortation to watch.

Living Jesus' Counsel in Mark 13

Today we are in the waiting time. We *Adventists*—who arose from the expectation of Jesus' return on October 22, 1844—are still here. How shall we then live until the Advent?

Sad to say, some are so frustrated over what they perceive to be a delay in Jesus' return that they are Adventists in name only. They hear sermons on the Second Coming, and join in the great chorus of the church, "We Have This Hope"; but the soon return of Jesus no longer shapes their lives in a significant way. They have become like the people described in Ezekiel 33:32—"Indeed, to them you are nothing more than one who sings love songs with a beautiful voice and plays on an instrument well, for they hear your words but do not put them into practice."

How different is the Adventist life sketched by Jesus in Mark 13! Here the Master portrays a people who eagerly await His coming, an anticipation that brightens even times of persecution and difficulty. They observe the times, which, like the fig tree, show that the end is near. And they maintain an attitude of watching and waiting, living on the knife-edge of time and leaning into the future, which is God's.

If some Adventists have suffered spiritual burnout, others fall into the opposite camp. They spend time and energy trying to figure out just *when* Jesus will some. Employing charts, calendars, and calculations, they arrive at a specific or implied date for the Second Coming.

But Jesus said, referring to the His second coming, "No one knows about that day or hour, not even the angels in heaven, nor the Son, but only the Father" (Matt. 24:36). After His resurrection the disciples inquired: "Lord, are you at this time going to restore the kingdom to Israel?" (Acts 1:6). His response: "It is not for you to know the times or dates the Father has set by his own authority" (verse 7).

Ellen White preached on Acts 1:6, 7 in a sermon in Lansing, Michigan, in 1891. As she had consistently counseled throughout her long ministry whenever Adventists began to get excited over dates for the Second Coming, she again warned against all such calculations. In effect, she said we have more important ways to spend our efforts—to live every day for the glory of the Master by building up His kingdom. And her words are still worth remembering in our day more than 100 years later: "You will not be able to say that He will come in one, two, or five years, neither are you to put off His coming by stating that it may not be for ten or twenty years" (*Selected Messages,* book 1, p. 189).

Eschatological fever draws a crowd and sells books. But it is unbiblical and irresponsible, because ultimately it leads to spiritual burnout after the dates pass without Jesus' return.

How then shall we live as we await the Advent?

Not in lifeless religion in which the coals of hope have grown cold.

Not in crystal-ball gazing and newspaper-headline scanning.

Not in retreating into isolated regions to live alone and wait alone.

Not in debate and arguing as to why Jesus hasn't come as we suppose He should have (with the attending finger-pointing).

No! But in loving, active service to others, sharing the "blessed hope" and ministering to the poor, the hungry, the downtrodden, the needy. In awaking every morning and praising God for the new day and for life with meaning and purpose. And in working at the post that He has given us, filling each moment with the hope, joy, and peace He puts within us.

How then shall we live?

By being persons who are fully alive—to His glory.

11

Crisis!
(Mark 14:1-52)

We come at last to the climax of Jesus' ministry. For this end was He born—born to die! He was "the Lamb slain from the foundation of the world" (Rev. 13:8, KJV). The manger in Bethlehem already contained a cross.

In one sense we are all born to die. Along with taxes, death is the great inevitable in human experience. "The living know that they shall die," as Ecclesiastes tells us (Eccl. 9:5, KJV). Because we come into a world cursed and blighted by the Fall of the race, our life is a one-act play—beautiful, often comic, but always tragic. Every life ends the same way in this drama.

But the Babe of Bethlehem would face death not as any human being before or since. He would confront death, wrestle it to the ground, and vanquish it. By His dying He would set humanity free; by His suffering He would release joy; and by His despair He would bring hope.

The moment of His dying would be at once tragic and glorious, combining defeat and victory, extinction and salvation. All history and all humanity held its breath then.

The last three chapters of Mark's Gospel focus on those hours, as do the final portions of all four Gospel accounts. In this chapter, covering Mark 14:1-52, we feel the rush of events as the gathering storm of hatred and opposition to Jesus reaches crisis point. Our next chapter will cover Mark 15 and will zero in on the day Jesus died: Good Friday, the climax of the ages. Then, taking up Mark 16, we shall consider the surprise ending, the denouement, to this greatest story ever told.

Intrigue

In considering the life of Jesus, especially its final events, we easily fall into the mistake of failing to give full weight to its grim reality. We have heard the Passion recited perhaps scores of times and even seen reenactments, and the very familiarity may cause us to think of it as merely a story. We know how the plot comes out, so the milestones toward the inevitable end assume an element of unreality, like a Hollywood production.

Further, Scripture makes clear that behind the scenes God was directing the drama to its appointed conclusion. As we already noted, three times in Mark's account Jesus tells His disciples point-blank that He will be betrayed, mocked, rejected, and killed in Jerusalem, but that He will rise again from the dead. Repeated references to events happening to fulfill prophecy add to the sense of divine inevitability in the Passion.

Let's be perfectly clear: the events of the Passion were terribly, grimly real for Jesus. Although God predicted what would happen, the risk of failure and eternal loss did not decrease one whit. Jesus struggled; Jesus was tested to the limit; Jesus could have quit; and Jesus could have failed.

Thus while the Father's eternal plan to win back a lost world worked itself out, every moment in the drama was pregnant with possibilities for good or bad choices. God was working out a divine plan, but other plans were also being hatched and put in place.

"The chief priests and the teachers of the law were looking for some sly way to arrest Jesus and kill him" (Mark 14:1). It had been their plan for some time. During the previous months their resolve had hardened. Without doubt the crowd's acclamation on Palm Sunday made them determined to act without delay. Time was running out. They had to put the upstart peasant from Galilee out of the way before He did more damage to their authority. Clearly Jesus threatened the whole religious establishment that centered in the Temple and that provided them with power and prestige.

So for the enemies of Jesus the question was not what to do, but how and when. Gladly would they have openly arrested Him, but that wouldn't have worked—Jesus had the support of the crowds. " 'But not during the Feast,' they said, 'or the people may riot' " (verse 2).

Their problem was that Jesus was constantly in the midst of a crowd. Each morning He walked into the city, and each evening He departed, and probably many other pilgrims—including those from Galilee—were doing the same thing. Nights Jesus spent outside the city, not in a village like nearby Bethany, where they might have tracked Him down, but in the open (see also John 7:53-8:1).

Then an unexpected solution fell into the hands of His enemies. One of His close associates sought them out and offered to make a deal. He would lead them to Jesus at a time and place away from the crowds. "Then Judas Iscariot, one of the Twelve, went to the chief priests to betray Jesus to them. They were delighted to hear this and promised to give him money. So he watched for an opportunity to hand him over" (Mark 14:10, 11).

The chief priests and scribes were planning their moves, and so did Jesus. He avoided exposing Himself to a quick, quiet arrest. Not only did He spend nights outside the city from Sunday through Wednesday, but when Thursday came He kept secret the location for the Passover meal.

The disciples, wondering what the plan was, asked Jesus, "Where do you want us to go and make preparations for you to eat the Passover?" Jesus' reply showed that He already had made a private arrangement: "Go into the city, and a man carrying a jar of water will meet you. Follow him. Say to the owner of the house he enters, 'The Teacher asks: Where is my guest room, where I may eat the Passover with my disciples?' He will show you a large upper room, furnished and ready. Make preparations for us there" (verses 13-15).

If Jesus had said, "Look for a woman carrying a jar of water," that would have been of no help. In that society *women* carried the water. But a man with a water jar? That would be a clear signal. Nor did Jesus tell them to say anything to the man. Rather, they were simply to follow him to the house where they would find the large upper room laid out for Passover.

Clearly Jesus had friends in Jerusalem, friends beyond the twelve. Individuals who would work secretly with Him to provide a place for Passover and keep it confidential.

John's Gospel sheds further light on the intrigue surrounding Jesus' time in Jerusalem. We read that on an earlier occasion "Jesus hid himself, slipping away from the temple grounds" (John 8:59), and that as Passover drew near, "the chief priests and Pharisees had given orders that if anyone found out where Jesus was, he should report it so that they might arrest him" (John 11:57).

In light of this cat-and-mouse aspect of the last days of Jesus' life, Judas' treachery becomes all the more reprehensible. No wonder Jesus' enemies were, as Mark says, "delighted" when he came to them (Mark 14:11).

What about this mole in Jesus' operation? Did he all along plan to betray his master, or did something happen to tip the scales?

Judas
The saddest words, it has been said, are "it might have been." How

true this was of Judas Iscariot! Admired by the other disciples, a standout in talent and abilities, he might have been the leader of the group. He might have become a powerful influence for good in the early church. And he might have had a Gospel or Epistle named for him in the New Testament. But we never will have a "Gospel of Judas" or letters of Judas. And think how the other apostles have given their names to thousands of baby boys in many lands—consider all the Peters, Johns, Jameses, Philips, and Matthews. But people do not name their children after Judas. That name, which might have been acclaimed in Christian history, has instead gone down in infamy.

Here is a quiz concerning Judas.

1. True or False? Hope still existed for Judas as he took part in the Lord's Supper.
2. When did Judas pass the point of no return in his spiritual life?
   A. When he first went to the priests and agreed to betray Jesus to them?
   B. When he left the upper room?
   C. When he hanged himself?
3. True or False? Judas expected Jesus to deliver Himself from His enemies.
4. Which of the following are true about Judas?
   A. He was the treasurer for the disciples.
   B. He was the most attractive candidate for leadership.
   C. He did not really believe in Jesus.
   D. He believed in Jesus but thought that He was too slow in asserting Himself as king of Israel.

And now the $64,000 question: Could *we*—could *I*—become a Judas? What can keep me from betraying the Lord?

I would answer the quiz as follows:

1. True. As Jesus washed Judas' feet, he must have been drawn toward the Master. And during the Supper, when He stated that one of the twelve would betray Him, Jesus still did not embarrass Judas by exposing him.
2. B—John tells us that when Judas, having fought back Jesus' loving appeal, left the Supper and went out, "it was night" (John 13:30). In my opinion, Judas sealed his fate by his decision to

reject Jesus and go to His enemies at that moment.

3. I think this is true. Judas' actions when Jesus was taken prisoner—regretting his actions and committing suicide—suggest that he did not think that the Master would permit Himself to be arrested.

4. A, B, and D are true. Scripture explicitly tells us that Judas kept the money bag (and helped himself to its contents [John 12:6]!). Further, he seemed on the surface to be the disciple most likely to succeed. His natural abilities led to his being made treasurer for the group. But Judas was too clever by half. In Galilee he had grown increasingly frustrated with Jesus' reluctance to assert Himself as Israel's king. Now, in Jerusalem, he thought the time was ripe for Jesus to act. Judas would force Him into a situation in which He would have to assert Himself to save Himself. At the end of the day, Judas thought, Jesus would emerge as King Messiah, and he would have a place of honor—plus be a little richer himself out of it all.

As for the final question: Could *I* become a Judas? The answer is yes. No one of us is immune from temptation, secure from falling. We can say that we follow Jesus and in fact do so, but we may lose our way. The apostle Paul realized that even after all his labors he could become a Judas: "Therefore I do not run like a man running aimlessly; I do not fight like a man beating the air. No, I beat my body and make it my slave so that after I have preached to others, I myself will not be disqualified for the prize" (1 Cor. 9:26, 27).

Wherein then is our hope? Not in ourselves, but in Jesus. By daily dying to our own will, strength, and plans, and casting ourselves upon Him. In Him alone are we safe—and we are safe there.

But let's go back to Judas. Can we identify any event that pushed him over the edge to disaster?

I think we can. Mark in his Gospel tells us about the plot to kill Jesus but the lack of opportunity (Mark 14:1, 2), then breaks to recount the story of the woman who poured the perfume on Jesus, and after that describes how Judas went to the chief priests and offered to betray Jesus to them. From that point on the story moves into the events of Thursday, leading up to the Master's arrest.

As you examine the way Mark puts his chapter 14 together, you get the sense that verses 3-9, which tell the story of the woman who anointed

117

Jesus, break the flow of the development of the plot against Jesus. They seem like an insert.

In fact, they are an insert—not from someone else, but from Mark himself. In the opening verse of the chapter Mark locates the time frame as "only two days away" from the Passover—that is, on Tuesday of the Passion Week. Since the story of the woman follows almost immediately, we might think that the incident occurred around the same time, but in fact it didn't. John locates the event precisely: it happened "six days before the Passover" at Bethany (John 12:1-8). This means that Mark's account backtracks in time at Mark 14:3 to bring in this story (he signals that he is doing so by telling us that the event took place in Bethany, not in Jerusalem).

What does Mark intend by his departure from chronological order? He wants us to see the links in the story of Jesus' passion. The account of the woman's anointing, which looks like an insertion that breaks the flow of the story, actually plays an important role. It gives us the reason for Judas' decision to go to the chief priests and scribes.

John makes clear that Judas was the disciple who strongly objected to Mary's act of love. Judas claimed to be concerned about the poor and the possible use of the expensive gift to help them, but he was actually a thief and a liar. Stealing from the money bag, he wasn't interested in the impoverished but in himself. Jesus' rebuke of the disciples for their mean-spiritedness hit home to Judas, who had voiced the objection. For him it was the last straw in months of disappointment and growing frustration over Jesus' failure to exert Himself as the popular political Messiah that he and the other disciples were waiting for.

The Last Supper

Jesus looked forward to the last meal with His friends. Luke's account tells us that the Master declared, "I have eagerly desired to eat this Passover with you before I suffer" (Luke 22:15). The "hour" that Jesus had spoken about many times and for which He now steeled Himself was about to break over Him. These moments with the twelve would be their last time together until after the Resurrection. And then, of course, the twelve would become the eleven—Judas would be no more.

The disciples knew nothing of all this. Although Jesus had repeatedly tried to prepare them for the crisis in Jerusalem, they remained confused, unable to break out of the shell of preconceived messianic notions.

"While they were eating, Jesus took bread, gave thanks, and broke it." Giving it to His disciples, He said, "Take it; this is my body" (Mark 14:22).

Then picking up the cup, He offered a prayer of thanks and handed it to them. They all drank from it, and Jesus said: "This is my blood of the covenant, which is poured out for many" (verse 24).

All four Gospels record Jesus' final meal with His friends. The accounts in Matthew, Mark, and Luke are quite similar. From John, however, we learn that Jesus washed the disciples' feet (John 13:1-17), and we find no mention of the "This is my body . . . this is my blood . . ." formula. As elsewhere, John apparently passes by information already noted in the three earlier Gospels and instead supplies additional details.

Luke's account of the Supper includes Jesus' admonition: "Do this in remembrance of me" (Luke 22:19), and the early Christians did celebrate the Last Supper. Some 20 years later Paul writes to Christians in Corinth, and his letter makes clear that they gathered together to observe the Lord's Supper (1 Cor. 11:20). However, Paul is displeased over their conduct at the Supper. They combined the actual Supper (the bread and the wine) with a more extensive meal, as Jesus did on that last Thursday night, but now some members ate royally while others had nothing. Paul counsels them to take their meal at home before the Supper and so avoid the abuse of Christian fellowship (verses 21-34).

The Last Supper has become a rite of the Christian church. Known as Communion, or the Lord's Supper, it is observed by almost all who take the name of Jesus (with few exceptions, such as the Salvation Army). In the large body of believers that in time became known as the Roman Catholic Church the Supper assumed major importance. By the end of the second century we can discern two trends converging: the movement to regard ministers of the gospel as priests, and the Lord's Supper—administered only by priests—as having sacramental value. In time the teaching of the Mass emerges full-blown, wherein the priest by pronouncing the words of the institution becomes creator of the Creator, as the wafer (bread) becomes—so it is taught and believed—the actual body of Christ and the wine His actual blood.

Did not Jesus say to the twelve: "This is my body. . . . This is My blood"? Indeed. But He obviously did not mean the words literally. Picture the scene—Jesus reclining around the table with His friends. When He breaks the bread and when He passes the cup, He is *there,* separate and apart from the bread and the wine. He and the twelve *know* that the bread isn't His body or the wine His blood. Instead, by partaking of them they are *choosing to identify themselves with Him in His passion.*

If we simply go back to that Thursday night and think through the scene and Jesus' words, we must realize how far from the original intent has become the teaching of the Mass.

Note 1 Corinthians 10:16—"The cup of blessing which we bless, is it not the communion of the blood of Christ? The bread which we break, is it not the communion of the body of Christ?" (NKJV). Consider also 1 Corinthians 11:23-26, which declares the bread and the wine to be a remembrance of the death of Jesus. The book of Hebrews argues emphatically that Christ died once for all—He is not sacrificed again and again every time someone celebrates the Lord's Supper. "Nor is he there to offer himself again and again, as the high priest enters the sanctuary year by year with blood not his own. If that were so, he would have had to suffer many times since the world was made. But as it is, he has appeared once and for all at the climax of history to abolish sin by the sacrifice of himself" (Heb. 9:25, 26, NEB).

Gethsemane

Just outside the eastern wall of Jerusalem, in the Kidron Valley, below the Mount of Olives, lies an orchard of olive trees. Its name, *Gethsemane,* means in Hebrew "olive press," and the garden probably had a press for extracting oil that lent its name to the site.

Jesus was a man of prayer. Throughout the Gospels we find Him communing with the Father, often spending the entire night in prayer. When He visited Jerusalem, the garden became for Him a retreat from the demands of the crowd and the intrigues of foes. It was a quiet place, a hallowed spot.

But on this Thursday night, this last night of the Savior's earthly life, He found no repose here. Gethsemane became for Him the "olive press" indeed as events crushed, squeezed, and wrung dry His soul.

Gethsemane—the word conjures up countless paintings, sermons, and meditations. Jesus' struggle in the olive grove outside Jerusalem just prior to His arrest has moved Christians for 2,000 years and still grips our interest today. Perhaps as nowhere else in the Gospels we here see the humanity of Jesus laid bare, His closeness to us. But we also sense mystery, as we wonder why He agonized to such an extent that night.

All four Gospel writers record the event, Matthew and Luke in accounts closely parallel to Mark's (Matt. 26:36-46; Luke 22:40-46) and John in a variant form (John 17:1-18:2). But we find another voice in the book of Hebrews, in which the writer (presumably Paul), who argues strongly for the true humanity of Jesus, observes: "During the days of Jesus' life on earth, he offered up prayers and petitions with loud cries and tears to the one who could save him from death, and he was heard because of his reverent submission. Although he was a son, he learned obedience from what he suffered" (Heb. 5:7, 8).

The language in Hebrews is very strong, both in translation and in the original Greek. Jesus did not pray silently: He pleaded with God through "loud cries and tears." We know what He prayed for, because even though the disciples kept dozing off, they couldn't help hearing His imploring words: "Abba, Father," "everything is possible for you. Take this cup from me. Yet not what I will, but what you will" (Mark 14:36).

Anyone who doubts whether Jesus was truly human, who thinks of Him as a superman, or who wonders if He knows how desperate we can feel at times, should go to Gethsemane. There you see Jesus of Nazareth stripped of divine power and authority, broken, pleading, anguishing.

Previously Jesus had spoken of His approaching death and had even said, "I have power to lay it [My life] down and I have power to take it again" (John 10:18, KJV). But that was *before* Gethsemane. Here in the garden He could only collapse to the ground and implore, "Abba, Father," "everything is possible for you. Take this cup from me" (Mark 14:36).

There it is—the cup! The cup of woe, separation, and desolation. The cup of feeling godforsaken. The cup of the sins of fallen humanity.

Once, when James and John came to Jesus seeking the best seats in the kingdom, He asked them, "Can you drink the cup?" (Mark 10:38). In their vain confidence they replied, "We can" (verse 39). But they could not. Only in part would they as followers of Jesus eventually share His experience.

Jesus' cup was His and His alone. Only He could drink it. Only He could become the sin-bearer for a lost world. And praise God, He *did* drink it. He lifted it high and drained it to the dregs, taking the last sin of the last sinner on Himself. Jesus, the book of Hebrews tells us, *tasted death* for everyone (Heb. 2:9).

In Gethsemane that cup trembled in the hands of a man—yes, the God-man, but a man nonetheless. His humanity shrank from the ordeal. He sought a way out, another way, any way—provided it was from God.

But there was no other way.

Of all the words written about Gethsemane, none lift the veil on its mystery and speak to my heart as do those of Ellen White in her chapter "Gethsemane" in *The Desire of Ages* (pp. 685-697). Consider the following example:

"Turning away, Jesus sought again His retreat, and fell prostrate, overcome by the horror of a great darkness. The humanity of the Son of God trembled in that trying hour. He prayed not now for His disciples that their faith might not fail, but for His own tempted, agonized soul. The awful moment had come—that moment which was to decide the destiny of the world. The fate of humanity trembled in the balance. Christ might even now refuse to drink the cup apportioned to guilty man. It was not yet too late. He might wipe the bloody sweat from His brow, and leave man to perish in his iniquity. He might say, Let the transgressor receive the penalty of his sin, and I will go back to My Father. Will the Son of God drink the bitter cup of humiliation and agony? Will the innocent suffer the consequences of the curse of sin, to save the guilty? The words fall tremblingly from the pale lips of Jesus, 'O my Father, if this cup may not pass away from me, except I drink it, thy will be done'" (p. 693).

Peter

When the crisis broke, all the disciples failed miserably.

Jesus in His hour of extremity sought the companionship and support of praying friends. But they slept.

He warned them that the hour of testing was upon them, that they needed to watch and pray. Instead they ignored His words.

The mob came and seized Jesus. His disciples deserted Him and fled.

Although all the disciples failed, Peter's performance was particularly sorry. At the Supper he had been so confident: "Even if all fall away, I will not" (Mark 14:29). And when Jesus told him that very night he would disown Him three times, the disciple brushed the possibility aside, asserting emphatically: "Even if I have to die with you, I will never disown you" (verse 31).

Yet he did. Within only a few hours, in fact, Peter's resolve collapsed like a sand castle swept away by a mighty wave. Confronted by a servant girl, he denied he knew Jesus, then repeated it again and again, eventually lacing his betrayal of the Master with profanity.

This was Peter at his worst. It is us at our worst. How quickly we make promises, and how quickly we break them. How fair are our words of loyalty to Jesus, but how base our actions of betrayal.

The beloved John was there in the upper room when Jesus had predicted that "you will all fall away" (verse 27). He joined the others in insisting that they would never desert Him (verse 31). But when they all turned their backs on Jesus in Gethsemane and fled, John ran away too.

But here's the difference between John and Peter: John entered the courtyard of the high priest—in fact, it was he who got Peter admitted (John 18:15, 16)—but he did not publicly deny Jesus. He did not try to conceal his association with his Master.

Peter's failure was a base act—no way to deny it. He, so often ready to speak for the rest, failed the rest. And above all, he failed his Master.

So far will self-confidence take us down the path of ruin. We think that we are strong enough to withstand the assaults of the enemy, that nothing could shake our loyalty to Christ. But we do not, cannot, foresee what even a day may bring forth. Only by living as Paul did—"I have been crucified with Christ and I no longer live, but Christ lives in me. The life I live in the body, I live by faith in the Son of God, who loved me and gave himself for me" (Gal. 2:20)—can we be guarded against denying the Master. And only as we realize and put into practice "for when I am weak, then I am strong" (2 Cor. 12:10) can Jesus supply grace sufficient for every situation.

Grace—that's the final word in Peter's story. He failed miserably, but Jesus brought him back. When the cock crowed and Jesus turned and looked at him, Peter broke down and wept (Mark 14:72).

Jesus brings hope to those who break down and weep. He offers us another start, a second chance.

Two betrayals in Mark 14: one man plotted with Jesus' enemies to betray Jesus, and did. One man never expected to betray Jesus—that was furthest from his intent—but also did.

One man ended a suicide.

The other died following his Lord, crucified as He was.

12

Calvary

(Mark 15:1-41)

All roads lead to Calvary—all roads ever built anywhere, at any time. Calvary is the focal point of history. Everything before converges toward it, and everything afterward lies in its shadow. It is, as the apostle wrote, "the end of the ages" (Heb. 9:26).

And it poses the supreme question of all time: Who was this man who died there? During the course of centuries the Romans crucified thousands, but this cross is different in some way. On that Friday—Good Friday to Christians, but bad Friday to two others—the crosses on either side of Jesus held impaled felons. We don't know their names, nor does history take notice of them. It's the cross in the middle—*His* cross—around which the drama swirls.

To believers, Calvary supplies the ultimate understanding of the ages. The answer to such vital questions as Who was Jesus of Nazareth? What is God like? What is good, and what is evil?

Secular history provides almost no information about Jesus. All that the Roman writers noticed about Him—and how slight it is—was that there had lived a Jew named Jesus, and that He was crucified when Pontius Pilate governed Judea.

Matthew, Mark, Luke, and John tell us far more. For each the events of Good Friday form the climax of the faith account of Jesus they have been developing. They do not attempt to minimize the story. Nor do they reveal any hint of embarrassment that the One they confess as Lord died as a common criminal or make any effort to excuse or explain what hap-

124

pened. Their tone foreshadows that of Paul: "But God forbid that I should glory, save in the cross of our Lord Jesus Christ, by whom the world is crucified unto me, and I unto the world" (Gal. 6:14, KJV).

The accounts of the Crucifixion in the four Gospels agree in the big picture but show individual variations in detail. By piecing the story together from all of them we learn that Jesus uttered seven sayings from the cross. Mark records just one, the wrenching " 'Eloi, Eloi, lama sabachthani?'—which means, 'My God, my God, why have you forsaken me?' " (Mark 15:34). He also tells us that Jesus gave a loud cry just before He expired (verse 37).

Quite possibly the first written of the four, Mark's account of Calvary carries a powerful impact. In simple, straightforward, unadorned language he tells us what happened that day. He doesn't interpret but simply relates the story and lets the reader decide what to do with it.

A parade of characters passes across the stage, and each of them invites our reflection. Pilate, the cruel official, who, strangely enough, became a saint in the Coptic tradition; Barabbas, who got off scot-free, in some ways a type of us; Simon of Cyrene, who carried Jesus' cross; the soldiers, who gambled for His clothing; the centurion, who watched over the scene and, observing how Jesus died, exclaimed: "Surely this man was the Son of God!" (verse 39)—the only human Mark identifies in his Gospel as using this expression of Jesus (everywhere else it's God and demons who call Jesus "Son of God").

But instead, let us turn our eyes on Jesus alone. "Some women were watching from a distance," Mark tells us (verse 40). Where were the disciples? We don't know. But the women stayed by. They watched as Jesus suffered and died, then observed as Jesus' body was placed in Joseph's tomb. Early Sunday morning they came to find the tomb empty. So we join them on that Friday, trying with them to understand what was happening.

What do they see? What does it all mean?

Golgotha

"They brought Jesus to the place called Golgotha (which means The Place of the Skull). Then they offered him wine mixed with myrrh, but he did not take it. And they crucified him" (verses 22-24).

The Romans did not invent the cross. That dubious honor probably belongs to the Phoenicians. But the Romans took it over and employed it for centuries to effectively deter opposition to their empire. They erected tens of thousands of crosses to enforce Roman rule.

The cross suited their purposes ideally. It was preeminently a means of public execution. They paraded the opponents of the Pax Romana through the streets carrying their cross or part of it. Passersby would see—and shudder. The place of execution itself was a public one. Let the crowds see the fate of anyone who dared to rise up against Rome! And death came slowly. The victim might linger for days, nailed or tied to the cross, until exposure and loss of body fluids finally brought merciful release.

The Romans employed the cross extensively—but never on their own citizens. No Roman citizen was ever to be crucified. When emperors occasionally ignored this restriction, widespread indignation and rioting resulted. The cross was a symbol of shame and humiliation—too horrendous for a citizen of Rome. The apostle Paul, for example, a Roman citizen, was not crucified. He was put to death with the sword.

But Jesus of Nazareth, lacking Roman citizenship, could be crucified—and He was.

"The spotless Son of God hung upon the cross, His flesh lacerated with stripes; those hands so often reached out in blessing, nailed to the wooden bars; those feet so tireless on ministries of love, spiked to the tree; that royal head pierced by the crown of thorns; those quivering lips shaped to the cry of woe.

"And all that He endured—the blood drops that flowed from His head, His hands, His feet, the agony that racked His frame, and the unutterable anguish that filled His soul at the hiding of His Father's face—speaks to each child of humanity, declaring, It is for thee that the Son of God consents to bear this burden of guilt; for thee He spoils the domain of death, and opens the gates of Paradise. He who stilled the angry waves and walked the foam-capped billows, who made devils tremble and disease flee, who opened blind eyes and called forth the dead to life—offers Himself upon the cross as a sacrifice, and this from love to thee. He, the Sin Bearer, endures the wrath of divine justice, and for thy sake becomes sin itself" (*The Desire of Ages,* pp. 755, 756).

A Roman Cross

"The written notice of the charge against him read: THE KING OF THE JEWS" (Mark 15:26).

The people had come out to watch Him die. Fishermen jostled for a place with merchants, and priests elbowed out housewives for a better view. Some knew Him well; others hardly at all. Many had come just to see the sight—to watch Him die. A number laughed and joked as the execution proceeded. A few wept—but they had to do it unobtrusively. The Romans would instantly crucify anyone who showed sympathy for the victim. The execution would take quite a while—certainly several hours—so they sat down on the grass and rocks to wait.

Soldiers were there too. Some of them stood on duty. After a while someone started a game of chance. An execution was nothing new to them—they had witnessed similar scenes many times before.

Yet this public dying was different. How could these people have known that before the day's end the officer in charge would declare, "Truly this man was the Son of God" (verse 39, KJV)? How could they realize that the execution they were carrying out would become the symbol of a new religion?

With the crowd we stare at Him as He hangs dying on the cross. We wonder, *How has He come to this?* "Stop this gross miscarriage of justice!" we want to shout out. "Who is responsible for this diabolical act?"

And as we watch Him, the answers come. Slowly. Four of them. Of course—the Romans were responsible! Those soldiers around the cross, that officer—all Roman. Roman authorities gave the orders for His death. They nailed Him to a Roman cross.

Legally, it is a Roman execution. The Jews did not execute by crucifixion. They stoned offenders to death. But first-century Palestine was under the subjugation of Rome, and the Jews no longer had authority to issue the death decree. "It is not lawful for us to put any man to death," they said to the Roman governor (John 18:31, KJV).

A Roman governor signed the death warrant. "Don't you realize I have power either to free you or to crucify you?" Pontius Pilate asked Jesus (John 19:10).

A Jewish Cross

"What shall I do, then, with the one you call the king of the Jews?" Pilate demanded of the crowd.

"Crucify him!" they shouted.

"Why? What crime has he committed?" Pilate insisted.

But they yelled all the louder, "Crucify him!" (Mark 15:12-14).

Jesus died on a Roman cross—but more was involved than just this. The Romans put Jesus to death, but they did so at the instigation of His own people. The cross of Jesus is more than a legal execution—it is a cross of rejection. "He came to that which was his own, but his own did not receive him" (John 1:11). When Pilate declared his innocence of the blood of Jesus, the crowd shouted out: "His blood be on us, and on our children" (Matt. 27:25, KJV). So the inscription on the cross, "The King of the Jews" (Mark 15:26), throbs with pathos.

But were the Jews Christ-killers? While their tragic rejection of Jesus as their king is a historic fact, did God then condemn them as a people, forever to bear their guilt, forever to suffer His curse?

When we turn back to the Gospel accounts of Jesus' crucifixion, some interesting data emerge. We notice such statements as these: "When the chief priests and the Pharisees heard Jesus' parables, they knew he was talking about them. They looked for a way to arrest him, but they were afraid of the crowd because the people held that he was a prophet" (Matt. 21:45, 46).

The enemies of Jesus laid plans to take Him by stealth. " 'But not during the Feast,' they said, 'or there may be a riot among the people' " (Matt. 26:5). And at the mockery of a trial before Pilate "the chief priests and the elders persuaded the crowd to ask for Barabbas and to have Jesus executed" (Matt. 27:20).

The members of the religious hierarchy had to persuade the population to support their demands. If we speak of Christ-killers, we should limit the term to the ecclesiastical leaders, not to the Jews as a people. The disciples of Jesus support such a view: "The chief priests and our rulers handed him over to be sentenced to death, and they crucified him" (Luke 24:20).

The death of Jesus, then, does not give theological warrant for anti-Semitism. And have we forgotten His own prayer from the cross: "Father, forgive them; for they know not what they do" (Luke 23:34, KJV)? Surely His own petition is not to remain eternally unanswered!

So we sit on the grass, looking up at the dying Jesus. The cross—His cross—is legally a Roman one. Religiously, it signifies His rejection by the leaders of His own people.

But as we continue to sit and watch, we realize that the cross represents even more. It is a divine cross.

A Divine Cross

"In the same way the chief priests and the teachers of the law mocked him among themselves. 'He saved others,' they say, 'but he can't save himself!' " (Mark 15:31).

When Pilate in the judgment hall boasted of his authority, Jesus gave him a surprising answer. "You would have no power over me if it were not given to you from above," He said (John 19:11). Also, in the Garden of Gethsemane at the time of His arrest—as the disciples prepared to defend Him—He commented, "Do you think I cannot call on my Father, and he will at once put at my disposal more than twelve legions of angels?" (Matt. 26:53).

Such ideas drastically alter our conception of the cross. It was clearly more than a miscarriage of Roman justice, more than a tragic Jewish failure. In some way God was very much in and behind the death of Jesus.

Jesus, in fact, expected the cross. Months before He bore it, He had spoken of His death at Jerusalem. Throughout His ministry He alluded to "his hour," or "my time" that was "not yet" (John 7:6, 30; 8:20, KJV). Constantly He looked forward to the final events of His life. As He entered upon His last week He knew what its end would be: "The hour has come for the Son of Man to be glorified," He said (John 12:23). And then—"But I, when I am lifted up from the earth, will draw all men to myself" (verse 32).

So in a sense neither the Romans nor the Jews killed Jesus. Neither Pilate nor the chief priests could have had power over Him unless He had permitted them.

Through the centuries the Romans erected tens of thousands of crosses. But this one stands alone in its uniqueness. It was an execution—but much more. God was working out a divine plan in the death of Jesus. "Christ died *for our sins*" was the affirmation of the first Christians (1 Cor. 15:3). He tasted death *for everyone*—so they believed and preached (Heb. 2:9, 10).

Now we begin to understand why the cross is shrouded in mystery—divine mystery. The physical sufferings, though intense, were the least of Jesus' woes. Acute mental and spiritual anguish battered His being. His agonizing cry of desolation—"My God, my God, why have you forsaken me?" (Mark 15:34)—was the cry of a soul that looks into the maw of eternal nonexistence.

So the cross is a divine one. Through its terrible suffering Jesus died vicariously. He was not being *punished* by God, for God had sent Him (John 3:16). Rather, through that cross God was "reconciling the world to himself" (2 Cor. 5:19).

The answers have come slowly as we have sat watching Jesus. They have surprised us. And the fourth is a shocker. Have we waited long enough to hear it?

My Cross

"For what I received I passed on to you as of first importance: that Christ died for our sins according to the Scriptures" (1 Cor. 15:3).

The apostle Peter declared of Jesus that " 'he committed no sin, and no deceit was found in his mouth.' When they hurled their insults at him, he did not retaliate; when he suffered, he made no threats. Instead, he entrusted himself to him who judges justly. He himself bore our sins in his body on the tree, so that we might die to sins and live for righteousness; by his wounds you have been healed" (1 Peter 2:22-24).

Where are the Romans? Where are the Jewish leaders? They do not come into view: only "our sins" appear here.

The entire New Testament teaches that Christ died for *our* sins, not for His own. Jesus is God's Lamb, "who takes away the sin of the world!" (John 1:29). He is God's expiation for sins when received by faith as a free gift (Rom. 3:21-25). And He is God's wisdom, whose cross is foolishness to the Greeks and a stumbling block to the Jews, but divine power to save all who believe (1 Cor. 1:18-25). Long before He came Isaiah had foretold Him as the Suffering Servant.

"Surely he took up our infirmities and carried our sorrows, yet we considered him stricken by God, smitten by him, and afflicted. But he was pierced for our transgressions, he was crushed for our iniquities; the punishment that brought us peace was upon him, and by his wounds we are healed. We all, like sheep, have gone astray, each of us has turned to his own way; and the Lord has laid on him the iniquity of us all" (Isa. 53:4-6).

Would we condemn the Romans? We must protest their flaunting of elemental justice in the death of Jesus. But we condemn ourselves, too.

Would we call the Jews Christ-killers? We grieve at their tragic rejection of Jesus. But we convict ourselves, too. Were they not representatives of us all? We would have done no better. Each of us would have crucified Him also. In fact, we *did* crucify Him! He died for *our* sins.

"Were you there when they crucified my Lord?" challenges the old spiritual. And now we know that we were. His cross is every person's cross—for everyone is a sinner.

And so—it is *my* cross! That is why the story of Calvary haunts humanity to this day. We see ourselves—I see *myself.*

But the good news of Christianity is that His cross *was* my cross. It no longer is mine. He took it—took it in its shame and disgrace, in its humiliation and despair. And because He did, He transformed it from a curse into a blessing; from darkness into light; from despair into hope; and from a symbol of death into one of life.

Who killed Christ? The biblical answer is almost too shocking—personally shocking—to repeat. I killed Christ!

But it does not leave me despairing. Because the cross is also the climax of a divine plan, it is my salvation. Through His death I find life.

"Why Have You Forsaken Me?"

"And at the ninth hour Jesus cried out in a loud voice, 'Eloi, Eloi, lama sabachthani?'—which means, 'My God, my God, why have you forsaken me?'" (Mark 15:34).

Although on earth people mocked and taunted the Man on the center cross, leaving just a few women to weep, in heaven the songs were hushed. The Father's heart suffered with the anguish of the Son, and angels looked on in wonder at the measures to which divine love would go in order to win back a lost world.

Around noon a strange darkness fell over Jerusalem. It was as though inanimate nature, suffering with its Creator, cast a veil over His final hours. Jesus was silent for a long while; then He uttered a terrible cry: "My God, my God, why have you forsaken me?" (verse 34).

Let those who assume that Christ could not have failed contemplate that moan from the cross. And let those who reason that Jesus' sufferings were not real because He was God and knew that everything would end in triumph contemplate it as well. It is the cry of someone forsaken by God, the sob of dereliction and despair.

And when the devil comes with his allurements, when the pleasures of sin excite our senses and the way of Jesus seems hard and dry, let us each remember that piercing wail from the darkness. Forever it tells how terrible is evil and how marvelous is the love of God.

Jesus, who had enjoyed unbroken communion with the Father, now felt forsaken. Why?

"Upon Christ as our substitute and surety was laid the iniquity of us all. He was counted a transgressor, that He might redeem us from the condemnation of the law. The guilt of every descendant of Adam was pressing upon His heart. The wrath of God against sin, the terrible manifestation of His displeasure because of iniquity, filled the soul of His Son with consternation. . . .

"Satan with his fierce temptations wrung the heart of Jesus. The Savior could not see through the portals of the tomb. Hope did not present to Him His coming forth from the grave a conqueror, or tell Him of the Father's acceptance of the sacrifice. He feared that sin was so offensive to God that Their separation was to be eternal. Christ felt the anguish which the sinner will feel when mercy shall no longer plead for the guilty race. It was the sense of sin, bringing the Father's wrath upon Him as man's substitute, that made the cup He drank so bitter, and broke the heart of the Son of God" (*The Desire of Ages*, p. 753).

The Loud Cry

"With a loud cry, Jesus breathed his last" (verse 37).

From John's account we learn that Jesus' last words were "It is finished" (John 19:30). What sort of utterance was this? Was it a groan of relief—"It's over at last"—or was it a triumphal declaration that Jesus had won the decisive battle for our salvation?

Surely the latter: "Christ did not yield up His life till He had accomplished the work which He came to do, and with His parting breath He exclaimed, 'It is finished' (John 19:30). The battle had been won. His right hand and His holy arm had gotten Him the victory. As a Conqueror He planted His banner on the eternal heights. Was there not joy among the angels? All heaven triumphed in the Savior's victory. Satan was defeated, and knew that his kingdom was lost" (*ibid.*, p. 758).

His last words on the cross have led evangelical Christians to speak of "the finished work of Christ." Some other Christians dislike this language because it can be used to set aside the ongoing high-priestly ministry of Jesus in the heavenly courts. However, in several senses we can legitimately comfort ourselves in the fact that Christ's parting shout signaled a decisive moment in time:

1. *On the cross Jesus offered up a complete, final sacrifice for sins.*

With that cry the veil of the Jerusalem Temple rent asunder. The system of sacrifices and offerings given anciently to Israel came to an end. All the multiplied deaths of animals in themselves could not atone for sin—they merely educated the people of God in the plan of salvation, pointing forward to the Lamb of God, who would take away the sin of the world (John 1:29).

We commemorate the dying of Jesus as we share in the Lord's Supper. But the bread and the wine are merely symbols to help us reenact Christ's last meal. They are not Christ's flesh and blood, for He died *once for all,* an all-sufficient sacrifice (Heb. 9:26, 28).

2. *The cross unmasked the character and intentions of the devil.*

The cross was Satan's final and most powerful weapon. He thought that the Majesty of heaven would never stoop to such humiliation. But He did, revealing the matchless power of love.

And thereby the devil exposed himself. He is a murderer and a liar who, despite his claims and deceptions, will stoop to any lengths to accomplish his ends.

3. *The cross sealed our salvation.*

The war goes on, but its conclusion is in no doubt. Christ won the decisive battle. Satan is a defeated foe. He wounded Christ's heel, but Calvary struck the deathblow to his head.

Praise God, "It is finished!" gives us strength in our struggles now and assurance of our eternal life in Him.

Forgiveness at the Cross

"And when the centurion, who stood there in front of Jesus, heard his cry and saw how he died, he said, 'Surely this man was the Son of God'" (Mark 15:39).

They bound Jesus, but they could not restrain His power to make men and women free. They nailed Him to a cross, but even as He hung dying He brought forgiveness to people around Him.

Consider the three men who found salvation in Him that day—Simon of Cyrene, the felon by His side, and the centurion.

Simon seemingly encountered Jesus by chance. He happened to be passing by when Jesus, hauling the crossbeam on the way to Golgotha, stumbled and fell beneath its weight. As Simon paused in sympathy, the soldiers conscripted him to carry the heavy beam.

By chance? No, God's timing is exquisite: He put Simon at that spot at that moment. And Simon not only relieved Jesus' burden but became a believer. Thus Jesus could take Simon's own burden and make him free.

The dying thief seemed the unlikeliest candidate for heaven. His life lay in ruins, with only a few grains of sand left in life's hourglass. Who could entertain hope for such a hardened criminal?

But God saw differently. Never write off any individual, no matter how hopeless he or she may appear, no matter how steeped in sin. If the felon on the cross could find salvation on Good Friday, so can *any* person we may meet. The power of Jesus' love, touching a human heart in its hour of extremity, can roll back the past and bring new life.

The stranger passing by, the criminal in his death throes, and even a Roman officer—Jesus brought forgiveness as He died.

"In the bruised, broken body hanging upon the cross, the centurion recognized the form of the Son of God. He could not refrain from confessing his faith. Thus again evidence was given that our Redeemer was to see of the travail of His soul. Upon the very day of His death, three men, differing widely from one another, had declared their faith—he who commanded the Roman guard, he who bore the cross of the Savior, and he who died upon the cross at His side" (*ibid.*, p. 770).

Jesus still forgives. That cross lifted high on Calvary will never lose its power. To men and women of every race and in every circumstance it offers hope and freedom today.

Have I found its power? Will I take up the cross today?

13

Risen Indeed!

(Mark 15:42-16:8)

O ne could hardly imagine a more unpromising basis for a new religion. The founder dies, executed as a common criminal and abandoned by His followers when the crucial test arrives. He perishes alone, forsaken by both humanity and by God. Whatever grand ideas He may have harbored about Himself or expressed to others, they obviously were a delusion. It's over.

No, it is not over, because His influence has only just begun. From the grave of this Man will sprout a new religion that will stretch out from Jerusalem to the north and south and east and west. It will become the most widespread and longest lasting of all faiths. The centuries will not dim the light of this Man and His message. Kings and kingdoms will rise and fall; ideologies will sweep across nations, flourish, and fade away; technologies, inventions, and discoveries will flow by; but this Man has not been, will never be, eclipsed.

In His teachings Jesus often told stories with a surprise ending. Sometimes He capped off the O. Henry-like close with the words: "So the first will be last, and the last will be first." His own story supplies the biggest reversal of all time. He who died the last of the last came out the First of the first. "Therefore God exalted him to the highest place and gave him the name that is above every name, that at the name of Jesus every knee should bow, in heaven and on earth and under the earth, and every tongue confess that Jesus Christ is Lord, to the glory of God the Father" (Phil. 2:9-11).

How could it be? What happened to make the story of Jesus of Nazareth stranger than any fiction—so amazing, so incredible, that it breaks the limits of human reason and experience and that ultimately you can only either accept it by faith or reject it as out of this world?

Jesus rose from the dead. He truly died on that terrible Friday and was pronounced dead by the Romans and believed to be dead by His followers. But on Sunday morning He was resurrected, leaving the tomb empty.

It wasn't a resuscitation. From time to time people who have been declared dead and are believed to be dead come back to life—after hours of immersion in cold water, for instance. They weren't dead—they only appeared to be. And with modern medical procedures others whose hearts stop beating are brought back to life. Staffs of emergency rooms specialize in reversing death.

But Jesus was resurrected, not resuscitated. The resurrection body differs markedly from our present bodies. Although He looked familiar to His friends as He conversed with them and even ate with them after His resurrection, He on at least two occasions suddenly appeared among them, even though they had locked the door of the room where they met (John 20:19, 26).

The resurrection is Jesus' crowning miracle. It shows that He was who He claimed to be—the Son of God. The terrible events of that Friday weren't just a travesty of justice and a despicable execution. Above all, it demonstrates that God approved of this "felon" who died between two thieves—approved Him indeed by the ultimate vindication of raising Him from the dead.

Every human story ends in a death—except for this Man's. For Him death was not the end but the prelude for a finale grand and breathtaking. His death was the greatest beginning of all.

The Resurrection is the beginning of our hope that death will not have the final word in our lives also. That, like Jesus, we too will return to life—not resuscitated, but resurrected with our individuality intact and in bodies that will never sicken, grow old, or die.

It was the beginning of a new religion, one with a message of hope for every son and daughter of Adam. A religion that contains teachings and embodies an ethic for daily living, but far more than that centers in the person of Jesus of Nazareth. A religion that does not try to hide the fact and details of that dreadful Friday but affirms that *in these very events* God was working out a divine purpose—the salvation of the world: "God made him who had no sin to be sin for us, so that in him we might become the righteousness of God" (2 Cor. 5:21). And a religion that confidently faces the future, that proclaims that the ancient enemy lies defeated, that because Jesus broke the bands of the grave and lives forever, we too shall live in Him.

Without Jesus' resurrection Calvary was a meaningless end to a good life. A dispirited band of followers had abandoned their Lord like rats from a sinking ship. Without Jesus' resurrection there is no message of hope. Death still reigns. And without Jesus' resurrection there would be no Christian church.

The Burial

As with other parts of the Jesus story, the four Gospel writers differ in details concerning the Resurrection but agree on the essential elements. Matthew alone tells us that an angel came down and rolled away the stone from the mouth of the tomb (Matt. 28:2-4) and that Jesus met with the remaining disciples on a mountain in Galilee (verses 16-20). Luke supplies the detail about the encounter on the road to Emmaus (Luke 24:13-35). From John's Gospel we learn of Jesus' appearance to Mary of Magdala (John 20:11-18), His exchange with doubting Thomas (verses 24-29), and the meeting after the disciples' fishing expedition (John 21:1-24).

In this chapter I shall focus on Mark's account. With each of the other Gospel writers contributing such interesting and vital details, it's hard to confine the discussion to Mark, but that is what we need to do to hear clearly *his* telling of the story. It is indeed a wonderful account as Mark relates it, but one with a surprising element, as we shall see.

As throughout Mark's Gospel, he tells what happened simply and straightforwardly, reporting rather than commenting. He lets the reader do the interpreting, catch for themselves the significance of what he is writing.

First, Mark tells what happened after Jesus uttered a "loud cry" and breathed His last (Mark 15:37). A new character enters the narrative: Joseph of Arimathea. We haven't heard of him before this, nor will we afterward. He steps into the limelight and plays a key role at a critical moment.

Jesus is dead, but He still hangs from the cross. According to Roman practice, people crucified for the crime of insurrection, as Jesus was, remained there for days after they died, their rotting bodies serving as a warning to any others who would dare defy mighty Rome. Only the governor could give the order for the body to be taken down earlier.

Neither Jesus' disciples nor His family members came forward. But Joseph of Arimathea did. No doubt he did so at some personal risk from both Roman authorities, who might have branded him as a fellow traveler and thus a dangerous person, and from the Jewish leaders, who would regard him as a secret sympathizer (which he in fact was). We do not know exactly what caused Pilate to grant Joseph's request: the fact that Joseph was a person of some prominence may have helped; or the Roman leader could have been feeling some pangs of conscience at his own role in the sordid events.

Mark tells us that it surprised Pilate to hear that Jesus was already dead. The Roman governor summoned the centurion to ascertain that it was so. Death by crucifixion often took several days, the victim eventually succumbing to the ravages of exposure, loss of bodily fluids, and pain. But Jesus died in only about six hours.

"So Joseph bought some linen cloth, took down the body, wrapped it in the linen, and placed it in a tomb cut out of rock. Then he rolled a stone against the entrance of the tomb" (verse 46).

All these details underscore one thing: Jesus really died. Joseph said He was dead. The centurion told Pilate that He was dead. Then Joseph prepared the body for burial, placed it in the rock-cut tomb, and rolled a large stone against the entrance. And further, we read that Mary Magdalene, Mary the mother of James, and Salome bought spices to anoint Jesus' body (Mark 16:1). The spices weren't for the purposes of preserving the body, but to mask temporarily the odor of decay. The women also believed that Jesus was dead—you don't anoint someone you expect to revive!

The point is elementary but so basic that it has to be hammered in: Jesus really died. He didn't faint and later revive in the coolness of the tomb, as some critics allege. Everyone who was there—the witnesses—affirmed that He was dead. Paul emphasizes this fact in his summary of the gospel: "For what I received I passed on to you as of first importance: that Christ died for our sins according to the Scriptures, that he was buried, that he was raised on the third day according to the Scriptures, and that he appeared to Peter, and then to the Twelve" (1 Cor. 15:3-5).

We should note another important fact that emerges from Mark's account: Jesus wasn't buried in secret. Joseph knew where Jesus' body was placed, as did the women who watched during the burial and came again on Sunday morning. (Matthew adds that the enemies of Jesus, apprehensive that something might happen to the body, posted a guard [Matt. 27:62-66].) So we can dismiss out of hand any theories that depend on the disciples' spiriting Jesus' body away, burying it secretly, and concocting the story about His coming back to life.

The Tomb Is Empty!

So to Sunday morning, and let us hear the story straight from Mark: "Very early on the first day of the week, just after sunrise, they were on their way to the tomb and they asked each other, 'Who will roll the stone away from the entrance of the tomb?' But when they looked up, they saw that the stone, which was very large, had been rolled away. As they entered the tomb, they saw a young man dressed in a white robe sitting on the right side, and they were alarmed. 'Don't be alarmed,' he said. 'You are looking for Jesus the Nazarene, who was crucified. He has risen! He is not here. See the place where they laid him. But go, tell his disciples and Peter, "He is going ahead of you into Galilee. There you will see him, just as he told you."' Trembling and bewildered, the women went out and fled from the tomb. They said nothing to anyone, because they were afraid" (Mark 16:2-8).

We can almost hear the women talking to one another as they make their way to the tomb in the early-morning light. They do not speculate as to whether they may somehow see Jesus again, nor do they expect to find His resting place in anything but the condition they had last seen it just before the Sabbath commenced.

Instead, their conversation involves a practical concern: How will they enter the tomb to anoint Jesus' body? Just before they left the scene on Friday evening they saw Joseph of Arimathea, likely assisted by servants, roll a large stone across its mouth. To reach Jesus' body they must first get into the tomb. The stone is too heavy for them to budge, but can they find someone to move it for them?

I admire these women. They showed unfailing devotion to Jesus, first in Galilee, then in Jerusalem. Peter and the others forsook their Lord, but not these women. Throughout the long hours of that dark Friday they stood and watched, suffering with Jesus on the cross, weeping with pain beyond words. What they did was risky. The Roman authorities could easily have crucified them for showing sympathy to someone being crucified as a traitor to Rome. But when He uttered the loud cry and breathed His last, they were still there. When Joseph came and took the body down from the cross, they followed and watched as he wrapped the corpse in the linen cloth, placed it in the tomb, and rolled the stone across the entrance. Only as the sun cast long shadows over the landscape did they finally leave.

But after the Sabbath—that is, Saturday night—they bought more spices to anoint the body. And now, by first light the next day, they gathered together and set out to perform this last act of devotion for the One they loved so much.

All others might have abandoned Jesus, but not they.

All others might be thrown into confusion and doubt, but not they.

And all others might be rethinking their relationship to Him, but not they.

They had loved Him once, and they loved Him still, despite everything that had happened and whatever the cost.

But they needn't have worried about the stone. As they drew near, they saw that it already had been rolled away. With mingled feelings of surprise and apprehension they entered the tomb. The body was gone! Instead of Jesus, they saw a young man dressed in white sitting on the right side of the tomb.

What could this mean? "Don't be alarmed," the angel said. "You are looking for Jesus the Nazarene, who was crucified. He has risen! He is not here. See the place where they laid him."

The angel continued: "But go, tell the disciples and Peter, 'He is going ahead of you into Galilee. There you will see him, just as he told you'" (verses 6, 7).

Galilee! On the Thursday night before His arrest Jesus had told the twelve: "After I have risen, I will go ahead of you into Galilee" (Mark 12:28). His words had seemed incomprehensible to them. Now the angel sends a message reminding them of what Jesus had said.

The angel's words in Mark 16:6, 7 contain three truths that lie at the heart of Christianity.

First, Jesus is risen. The tomb is empty—the body has disappeared. He had been placed in the tomb, but He has come back from beyond the river of death.

Second, the risen Lord extends forgiveness to the cowardly bunch who abandoned Him when He most needed them. And especially to Peter, natural leader of the group, but ultimately the biggest failure of them all. "Tell . . . Peter"—what a thoughtful, compassionate addendum to the message. Tell Peter that I have not abandoned him, even though he abandoned Me. Tell Peter I want to meet him. Tell him to go to Galilee, because we have an appointment there.

I am Peter. Perhaps, dear reader, you are too. Although we may make great professions, we do not walk the talk. But praise God, the risen Christ still calls us by name, singling us out to meet with Him.

Third, the risen Lord calls us to share the story with others. Mary of Magdala, Mary mother of James, Salome—tell the disciples and Peter the good news that Jesus is risen. Disciples and Peter, proclaim the good news that Jesus is risen. Followers of Jesus in these days, announce to the world that the tomb is empty, that Jesus the Nazarene has risen from the dead, and that He offers hope and forgiveness to all and the privilege of sharing with others the good news.

Then Mark records: "Trembling and bewildered, the women went out and fled from the tomb. They said nothing to anyone, because they were afraid" (Mark 16:8). It was all too sudden and too much for them—the stone rolled away, the body gone, the young man and his startling message. On the way to the tomb they had conversed with one another, but now they hurried away in silence. They were awestruck and bewildered, afraid and trembling.

And it reminds us of how Mark's story of Jesus began. As Jesus starts to teach and heal, it fills His hearers with wonder and amazement. "What is this?" they ask (Mark 1:27). "We have never seen anything like this!" (Mark 2:12).

Jesus, man of wonder, confounds people at the outset and to the very end.

The Close of Mark's Gospel

Thus far we can be certain that we possess the story of Jesus as John Mark penned it. But after Mark 16:8 the questions multiply.

The New Testament is the best-attested example of any literature from ancient times. True, we do not have the "autographs"—the original words written by Mark, Matthew, Luke, John, Paul, Peter, James, or Jude. But we have a treasure trove of ancient manuscripts, with one fragment dating from early in the second century A.D. Besides old manuscripts in the original Greek, we have early translations, plus portions of Scripture in "lectionaries" (similar to the Scripture readings at the close of our hymnal).

This large volume of ancient material enables scholars to recover with a high degree of certainty the original text of the New Testament writings. People wrote the New Testament by hand and copied—and copied and copied—it by hand right down to the invention of movable type in the fifteenth century. Inevitably, mistakes crept in: spelling errors, a word left out, a line missing, and so on. Occasionally, the scribes made a deliberate change, seeking to make clear something that didn't sound right or that didn't (to them) ring true theologically. So the manuscripts show many variations, the great majority of them trivial in nature. But because the volume of material is so large, scholars can trace the origin of a "mistake" in an early manuscript to its perpetuation in later manuscripts. With few exceptions the older the manuscript, the more reliable its text.

Now, to the Gospel of Mark. There is no question about the text through Mark 16:8, but after that point we enter an area of high uncertainty. The ending found in Mark 16:9-20 does not appear in the oldest and best Greek manuscripts, nor do the "fathers" of the church from the first four centuries regard these verses as coming from the hand of Mark.

On the other hand, we find another ending to the Gospel attached to some early manuscripts. These verses come after Mark 16:8: "But they reported briefly to Peter and those with him all that they had been told. And after this, Jesus himself sent out by means of them, from east to west, the sacred and imperishable proclamation of eternal salvation" (RSV).

Does this sound like Mark's voice? Even in translation the words jar: someone else is writing. The contrast is even greater in the original Greek.

So how did Mark wrap up the story of Jesus? We can't know for sure. It's possible that he wrote the words listed under verses 9-20. *The Seventh-day Adventist Bible Commentary* discusses the question and, while acknowledging the difficulties involved, opts for holding to these verses (see vol. 5, pp. 658, 659).

I am not so sure. Apart from the weak manuscript support, the passage, to me, bears the marks of something added on by another hand, by someone who felt that to end at verse 8 was too abrupt and that the book needed a "proper" ending.

And there's another reason. Only in this questionable material do we find these words purportedly from the risen Jesus: "And these signs will accompany those who believe: In my name they will drive out demons; they will speak in new tongues; they will pick up snakes with their hands; and when they drink deadly poison, it will not hurt them at all; they will place their hands on sick people, and they will get well" (Mark 16:17, 18).

The passage has led to some strange aberrations of Christianity. In the mountains of West Virginia, to this day some who claim the name of Jesus catch rattlesnakes and pass them by hand along the pews in worship service. For them, the ability to survive this bizarre practice "proves" that they are true believers. I find the custom and the theology behind it repulsive: it is a far cry from the experience of the apostle Paul, who survived an encounter with a venomous snake, not by intention but in the course of Christian service (see Acts 28:3-6).

What then are the options for the end of Mark?

1. Mark wrote it all, including Mark 16:9-20. This may, after all, be the correct answer to the problem.
2. Mark wrote an ending after verse 8, but it became lost. Sensing the

incompleteness of the work, someone in the second century wrote the ending we know as verses 9-20. And someone else in the second century wrote the different, shorter ending we mentioned above. In fact, we find other attempts at an ending in later centuries.

3. Mark intended his Gospel to close at Mark 16:8. Because such an ending seems abrupt, many readers of the Gospel, from the second century to today, think that he must have composed more. But some scholars, carefully tracing Mark's story as a whole, think it is just possible that Mark decided to wrap up the story right there, leaving the reader amazed and awestruck like the women.

I think they are right. Mark tells us from his opening line that his book will be about "Jesus Christ, the Son of God." What better way to close? Not a word wasted, case closed—and the reader, on the edge of the chair, forced to answer Jesus' searching query: "But who do you say I am?"

The Last Word

Whether or not we know how Mark concluded his Gospel does not change his last word. Even if we stop at Mark 16:8, which is unquestionably authentic, Mark has told us that Jesus, the one betrayed, sentenced to die, abandoned, crucified, dead and buried—*that* Jesus rose from the dead, vindicated by God to be what He claimed to be: Israel's true Messiah and the Son of God.

The Gospel writer tells us the tomb was empty, and further, that Jesus—the risen Lord—would meet with His disciples in person. These are the identical lines of evidence for the Resurrection presented by Matthew, Luke, and John. All describe the tomb as empty, and all record different encounters of Jesus with other individuals.

We who believe can add a third line of evidence that Jesus is alive. Perhaps it is really an extension of the second set above. It is this: We know that Jesus rose from the dead because He meets with us personally. Although we cannot see Him, as did Mary Magdalene; hear His voice, as in the case of Cleopas and his companion on the road to Emmaus; or touch Him, as Thomas did, He is just as real, the meeting is just as real, and the conversation is just as real.

The witness of our lives resonates with the experience of His first followers. Jesus is alive! We follow, not a Teacher long dead and gone, but One who, though dead indeed, burst out of the prison house of death. Jesus is alive!

Yes, the same Jesus who showed compassion to the men and women of Galilee showers compassion today on you and me. Jesus is alive!

The same Jesus who brought hope and healing to men and women back then brings hope and healing to you and me. Jesus is alive!

The same Jesus who forgave and made people whole still forgives and makes you and me whole. Jesus is alive!

This is Jesus, conqueror of Satan, victor over death.

This is Jesus, alive forevermore!

This is Jesus, the Son of God!